Classics In
Child Development

Classics In
Child Development

AN EXPERIMENTAL STUDY OF THE EIDETIC TYPE

BY

HEINRICH KLÜVER

ARNO PRESS

A New York Times Company

New York — 1975

Reprint Edition 1975 by Arno Press Inc.

Reprinted from a copy in
  The Clark University Library

Classics in Child Development
ISBN for complete set: 0-405-06450-0
See last pages of this volume for titles.

Manufactured in the United States of America

Library of Congress Cataloging in Publication Data

Klüver, Heinrich, 1897-
   An experimental study of the eidetic type.

   (Classics in child development)
   Reprint of the 1926 ed. published in Worchester,
Mass., which was issued as v. 1, no. 2 of Genetic psy-
chology monographs.
   Bibliography: p.
   1. Eidetic imagery. I. Title. II. Series.
III. Series: Genetic psychology monographs ; v. 1,
no. 2.
BF367.K535 1975   153.3'2   74-21418
ISBN 0-405-06468-3

$7 per annum
Single Nos. $2.00

March, 1926
Vol. 1, No. 2

GENETIC PSYCHOLOGY MONOGRAPHS

MARCH, 1926

AN EXPERIMENTAL STUDY OF THE EIDETIC TYPE[1]

BY

HEINRICH KLÜVER*

Department of Psychology of the University of Minnesota

[1]The writer gratefully acknowledges his indebtedness to Dr. W. R. Miles, Stanford University, for criticism and suggestions in the preparation of this paper.
*Transmitted to the Editors by K. S. Lashley, October 1, 1925.

AN EXPERIMENTAL STUDY OF THE EIDETIC TYPE

Heinrich Klüver

Department of Psychology of the University of Minnesota

I. *SURVEY OF PREVIOUS EIDETIC INVESTIGATIONS*

The following study represents an experimental investigation of the eidetic type.[2] To make clear the relationship of this work to the investigations of other experimenters a short survey of the papers published by E. R. Jaensch and his pupils will be necessary. Jaensch first systematically dealt with the problems centered around

---

[2] So far as I know it is the first eidetic study made in America. A preliminary report has been given at the meeting of the Western American Psychological Association, Aug. 1924: "Description of eidetic phenomena." Comp. Psychol. Bull. 1925, *22*, 331.

Note: E—Experimenter, S—Subject, AI—after-image, AB—Anschauungsbild, MI—Memory-image, I—Image.

In general, a, b, c, etc., in our records always designate two successive experiments on the S. The words given in quotation-marks are always statements of the S, the words in brackets refer to the E. The time given first is always the exposure time. Figures following the dash equal the time of duration of the I. This time, however, is not given in all instances. Ad lib(itum) means that the S is allowed to look at the object as long as he wants.

The results of this study are not based upon the records included; these records simply *illustrate* the various aspects of eidetic phenomena.

the eidetic type and our short survey will bring out the special character and the importance of these problems.

"Eidetiker" are individuals who possess or are gifted with optical "Anschauungsbilder."[3]   The aim of the Marburg school is to determine exactly the characteristics of these AB. It is not possible here—even not by means of a condensed summary—to show how far they succeeded. Only a provisional delimitation of AB—and, of course, at the same time of "Eidetiker"—can be given. P. Busse[4] states: "Unter subjektiven Anschauungsbildern versteht man die Fähigkeit, einen Sinneseindruck nach kürzerer oder längerer Zwischenzeit mit sinnlicher Deutlichkeit zu reproduzieren, z.B. eine optiche Vorlage im ganz eigentlichen und wörtlichen Sinne wieder zu 'sehen'." Thus one may *illustrate* the general structure of these phenomena by referring to the positive or negative after-images (AI). Similar definitions of AB appear in the publications of the other collaborators of the Marburg Institute. Bernhard Herwig[5] circumscribes the AB as follows: "The 'Anschauungbild' is a subjective visual phenomenon which is found in many young people, but

---

[3]Warren, H. C.: *"Some unusual visual after-effects,"* Psychol. Rev., 1921, *28*, p. 453, translates this term with "visualizations," English, Psych. Bulletin, 1921, *18*, with "percept-images."   Neither translation seems to be quite satisfactory. We therefore use the German word "Anschauungsbild."   (AB)

[4]Busse, P.: *Über die Gedächtnisstufen und ihre Beziehung zum Aufbau der Wahrnehmungswelt.*   Zsch. f. Psychol., 1920, *84*, 1.

[5]Herwig, B.: *Über den inneren Farbensinn der Jugendlichen und seine Beziehung zu den allgemeinen Fragen des Lichtsinns.* Zsch. f. Psychol., 1921, *87*, 129.

not so often among adults; if *e.g.*, a person gifted with AB is asked to look attentively for a while at an object —regardless whether it is two- or three-dimensional— this person sees the object again either when he closes his eyes or looks at a ground which serves as a background for the image." Oswald Kroh[6] defines the AB as "gewisse Vorstellungsbilder von halluzinatorischer Deutlichkeit, mit anderen Worten: besondere Formen empfindungsmässiger Vorstellungen," (*i.e.*, certain images of an hallucinatory clearness, in other words: special forms of perception-like images.) Kroh's definition practically coincides with Urbantschitsch's determination of "subjektive optische Anschauungsbilder."[7] Emphasis is laid upon the fact that the Eidetiker are able "einen dargebotenen Gegenstand, entweder nur unmittelbar nach der Betrachtung oder auch nach längerer Zwischenzeit, im buchstäblichen Sinne wieder zu sehen."[8]. Sometimes an exposure is not necessary; "also spontaneous images

---

[6]Kroh, O.: *Eidetiker unter deutschen Dichtern.* Zsch. f. Psychol., 1920, *85*, 118.

Kroh, O.: *Subjektive Anschauungsbilder bei Jugendlichen. Eine psychologische-pädagogische Untersuchung.* Göttingen: Vandenhoeck & Ruprecht, 1922, pp. VIII+195.

Kroh, O.: *Subjektive optische Anschauungsbilder bei Jugendlichen.* Zsch. f. päd. Psychol., 1922, *23*, 40.

Kroh, O.: *Die eidetische Anlage bei Jugendlichen.* Zsch. f. Kinderforschung, 1924, *29*, 63.

[7]Urbantschitsch, V.: *Ueber subjektive optische Anschauungsbilder.* Leipzig und Wien: F. Deuticke, 1907, pp. VI+211.

[8]Jaensch, E. R.: *Zur Methodik experimenteller Untersuchungen an optischen Anschauungsbildern.* Zsch. f. Psychol., 1920, *85*, 37.

occur."[9]   The definitions of AB found in other Marburg publications hardly differ from those just quoted.[10]   H. Zeman (Vienna)[11] modifying Fischer-Hirschberg's[12] definition characterizes the whole field of subjective optical AB (s. o. AB) very completely in the following way: "S. o. AB sind opt. Gedächnisbilder, die spontan oder willkürlich, oft unmittelbar nach Betrachten eines Gegenstandes, oft aber auch erst oder wieder nach Minuten, Stunden, Jahren, bei geschlossenem, in vielen Fällen auch bei offenem Auge auftreten, die in ausgesprochenen Fällen ein Bild des Gegenstandes urbildmässig gefärbt, zuweilen auch in grauer oder komplementärer Farbe wiedergeben, und die das Individuum buchstäblich sieht, ohne dass es deswegen dabei—in den allermeisten Fällen wenigstens—an die Realität eines in der Aussenwelt befindlichen Gegenstandes glaubt."

---

[9]Jaensch, W.: *Ueber psychophysische Konstitutionstypen*, Monatssch. f. Kinderheilkunde, 1921, 22, Helt 2.

[10]Gösser, A.: *Ueber die Gründe des verschiedenen Verhaltens der einzelnen Gedächtnisstufen.* Zsch. f. Psychol., 1921, *87*, 97.

Jaensch, E. R.: *Die experimentelle Analyse der Anschauungsbilder als Hilfsmittel zur Untersuchung der Wahrnehmungs—und Denkvorgänge..* Sitzungsberichte der Gesellschaft zur Beförderung der gesamten Naturwissenschaften zu Marburg, 1917.

Jaensch. E. R.: *Ueber die subjektiven Anschauungsbilder.* Bericht über den VII. Kongress für exp. Psych. in Marburg, 1922.

[11]Zeman, H.: *Verbreitung und Grad der eidetischen Anlage.* Zsch. f. Psychol., 1924, *96*, 209.

[12]Fischer, S. & Hirschberg, H.: *Die Verbreitung der eidetischen Anlage im Jugendalter und ihre Beziehungen zu körperlichen Merkmalen.* Zsch. f. d. ges. Neurol. u. Psychiat., 1924, *88*, 241.

A closer analysis of the works of the Marburg school*
brings out quite a number of descriptive and functional
criteria of the AB. (See Koffka's distinction between
"Deskriptionsbegriffe" and "Funktionsgriffe[13]"). It must
be noticed, however, that all these investigations are directed by a certain theory. The point of departure is not
only "eine bestimmte Auffassung vom Wesen der wissen-
schaftlichen Philosophie," but also a *psychological* theory
which they seek to prove experimentally. To get a better understanding of the presuppositions and the trends
of the school some points in the history of the investigations might be referred to.

E. R. Jaensch, a pupil of G. E. Müller, was in his previous work chiefly concerned with "problems of the
classical theory of perception."[14]

Urbantschitsch's book about visual AB appeared in
1907.[15] Two years later Jaensch (op. cit. pp. 386-388)

---

*The author has given the same presentation of the
views of the Marburg School in another context. Compare 59.

[13]Koffka, K.: *Zur Analyse der Vorstellungen und
ihrer Gesetze.* Leipzig: Quelle & Meyer, 1912, pp. VI
+392.

[14]Jaensch, E. R.: *Zur Analyse der Gesichtswahrneh-
mungen. Experimentell-psychologische Untersuchungen
nebst Anwendung auf die Pathologie des Sehens.* Zsch.
f. Psychol., 1909, Ergänzungsband 4.

Jaensch, E. R.: *Ueber die Wahrnehmung des Raumes.
Eine experimentell-psychologische Untersuchung nebst
Anwendung auf Ästhetik und Erkenntnislehre.* Zsch. f.
Psychol., 1911, Ergänzungsband 6.

[15]Cf. his earlier *"Ueber die Beeinflussung subjektiver
Gesichtsempfindungen."* Arch. f. d. ges, Physiol., 1903,
94, 347.

unable to accept the view that AB are merely of pathological nature, pointed out that the investigation of AB might become of central importance for general psychology. V. Urbantschitsch sharply distinguished two classes of visual memory-images: 1. "die einfache Vorstellung an das Gesehene," 2. "die anschaulichen Gedächtnisbilder," (*i.e.*, 1. the ordinary visual memory-image, 2, the perceptual memory-image.) He believes the latter phenomena are found especially among "youths and more easily excitable persons"; he would not hold, however, that all young people possess these AB. Urbantschitsch as an otologist was very much interested in the effect of disturbing stimuli upon AB.

We may briefly refer to some of his observations which the reader, however, must not take as entirely typical for the behavior of AB as generally observed in the psychological laboratory. For instance: the S has an AB of a certain picture. Various tones are then presented -C_1, left ear: the AB disappears, right ear: the AB grows pink—c^4, left ear: two dogs and a boy, previously invisible, appear, right ear, the whole AB becomes more distinct—C_1 and c^4, left ear: the girl before the house becomes much bigger, etc. (For further details see 97, p. 165).[16] Another example: the right eye sees the AB of the word *Aurgzet*. After having exposed the left eye to light the word *"Auge"* appears to the right; the letters

---

"*Ueber Sinnesempfindungen und Gedächtnisbilder.*" Arch. f. d. ges. Physiol., 1905, *110*, 437.

See also: "*Ueber subjektive Hörerscheinungen und subjektive optische Anschauunbsbilder.*" 1908.

[16]The number in brackets always refer to the number of the bibliography.

r, z, and *t* have disappeared. After the right eye's exposure to light the word *"Arzt"* appears to the left. The letters *u, g,* and *e* have disappeared. After a short time the letters *Aurgzet* reappear in a vertical position. C_{-1}, right ear: to the left *"Arzt"* appears; c_4, left ear: to the right *"Auge"* and *"Arzt"* appear one above the other, *Auge,* having a round *A, Arzt* a pointed one as it was in the material presented. (*Cf.* 97, p. 203). In general to test the modifiability of the AB, Urbantschitsch chiefly used the sounds of tuning-forks applied to the right or left ear, a compression of the jugular blood-vessels, and the galvanic current. In addition to these stimuli a reflecting mirror was used to cast light upon the closed eyes. Sometimes cold or warmth were applied to the cheeks or to the forehead.

It was natural that in discussing "psychonomic and apsychonomic influences upon the mechanism of reproduction," G. E. Müller in 1913[17] should refer to Urbantschitsch's investigation in order to show the influence of apsychonomic factors, *i.e.,* the influence of metabolism and of the anatomical-physiological constitution. From about the year 1910 Jaensch stimulated his students and assistants to look for persons gifted with AB. Thus it happened in 1917 that O. Kroh who was teaching in one of the Marburg high-schools discovered that AB are very frequent and quite normal phenomena at a certain age. Very elaborate researches have been carried on since that time. In 1923 Jaensch replying to a very sharp critique

---

[17]G. E. Müller: *Zur Analyse der Gedächtnistätigkeit und des Vorstellungsverlaufs.* III. Teil, 1913.

of Koffka[18] which accuses the Marburg school of having "insufficiently and inexactly investigated" the facts could point out that his conclusions are based upon six years' intensive and extensive work with the youth of a whole town.[19]

Special attention must be paid to certain points which the investigations of these six years stress again and again. In my opinion four points are particularly important:

1. It is claimed that eidetic investigations have "the importance of a *struktur*-psychological demonstration."[20] That is to say, since "the eidetic stage is to a certain extent a normal stage of development"[21] and since the investigations have shown that certain essential and permanent characteristics of the fully developed consciousness are more distinct in the preceding developmental stage, genetic psychology must begin not with protists, anthropoids or infants, but with that stage hitherto overlooked—with the eidetic stage. Herwig (27, p. 132) states that among 205 boys in Marburg,—10-14.5 years —76 boys, *i.e.*, 37% were found to be gifted with visual

[18]Koffka, K.: *Ueber die Untersuchungen an den sogenannten optischen Anschauungsbildern.* Psych. Forschung, 1923, *3*, 124.

[19]Jaensch, E. R.: *Ueber Gegenwartsaufgaben der Jugendpsychologie.* Zsch. f. Psychol., 1924, *94*, 38.

[20]Jaensch, E. R.: *Der Umbau der Wahrnehmungslehre und die Kantischen Weltanschauungen.* Zsch. f. Psychol., 1923, *92*, 1.

[21]Jaensch, E. R.: *Uebergang zu einer Schichtenanalyse des Bewusstseins und einiger seiner Substrate, gegründet auf die Strukturanalyse der eidetischen Entwicklungsschicht.* Zsch. f. Psychol., 1922, *91*, 83.

AB. (See also Krellenberg 66, p. 59: he refers to school classes with 32%, 26%, 28%, 46%, 17%, 34%, 67%, respectively). And H. Freiling (15) reports that in Ilsenburg Jaensch has found "40-50% very pronounced cases." A thorough investigation of a class of 38 boys having an average age of 12.4 years, revealed the fact that there were only 5 boys without AB[22].

The determination of the frequency of the eidetic disposition is the object of some more recent studies. In Breslau, Fischer-Hirschberg (14) found 99.3% (139 Eidetike among 140). The acme of the eidetic gift was found to be between the twelfth and fourteenth year. In Vienna, H. Zeman found 88% (176 Eidetiker among 200). The acme was during the pre- and postpubertal period. In Breslau as well as in Vienna a superiority of the female sex was discovered. The percentages, however, change considerably if the "latent" Eidetiker of Gottheil (21) are excluded. In this case we have practically the same percentage in Vienna as found by Kroh in Marburg: 61%; for Fischer-Hirschberg there remain 89.3%.

Kroh[23] found 7% among adults. But even Jaensch believes that not every child passes through the eidetic stage; there always will be cases where one finds no trace of AB even "with the most accurate methods of investigation." The cases we have, however, suffice for

---

[22]Jaensch, E. R. and W.: *Ueber die Verbreitung der eidetischen Anlage im Jugendalter.* Zsch. f. Psychol., 1921, *87*, 91.

[23]Kroh, O.: *Subjektive optische Anschauungsbilder bei Jugendlichen.* Zsch. f. päd. Psychol., 1922, *23*, 40.

him to make the eidetic investigations serviceable to the "Strukturanalyse des Bewusstseins" above referred to.

2. It is claimed that the same laws hold for eidetic phenomena and the phenomena of normal perception, *i.e.,* that the laws for eidetic phenomena are only "quantitatively different." Starting from this presupposition Jaensch thinks that eidetic investigations furnish the explanation of certain problems of general psychology. The problems of perception with which he was previously concerned are *now* investigated with Eidetiker and the interpretation, *e.g.,* concerning localization, horopter, contrast, etc., in the AB is applied to the corresponding phenomena in normal perception. Jaensch considers this standpoint to be justified because of the "psychonomic" behavior of the AB observed by him. In 1918 Stumpf[24] had expressed not only his skepticism concerning the soundness of Urbantschitsch's experiments but also "das allergrösste Misstrauen gegen die wissenchaftliche Beobachtungsfähigkeit der benutzten Versuchspersonen."

That implies that Urbantschitsch's material renders Jaensch's methodological presupposition untenable. Jaensch, however, states that he found only three cases among far more than 100 subjects "who in point of apsychonomy stand near to the observers of Urbantschitsch." All his conclusions are based on psychonomic cases, the other ones are—neglected in order to be subjected "to a special consideration." This seems to be the point of view even in the recent publications of the Marburg school.

---

[24]Stumpf, C.: *Empfindung und Vorstellung.* Abh. d. Preuss, Akademie d. Wissenschaften, 1918. Philos.-Historische Klasse.

3. Since on the one hand AB are apparently in some respect similar to AI while, on the other hand, they seem to show a certain relation to MI it is to be expected that Jaensch should aim at drawing a sharp line of demarcation between AI, AB and MI. The determination of AB concerning color, size, intensity, "weight", detail, relation to background, the conditions of arousal and disappearance, the degree of plasticity and flexibility, the degree of coherence, the degree of invariance, the relation to distracting stimuli is made *with reference* to AI and MI. One is primarily interested in the phenomena intermediate between AI and MI presupposing that for the purpose of eidetic investigations we are well enough informed about the characteristics of AI and MT. Again and again the statement is repeated that AI, AB and MI are three grades of memory ("Gedächtnisstufen"). Thus we have a hierarchy of grades of memory, (Krellenberg, Busse a. o.) the lowest of which is the AI and the highest grade the MI. It is denied that the functions of memory *teleologically* united form a homogeneous unity in so far as their *psychological* structure is concerned. Thus we have *"memories"*: a memory of AI, a memory of AB, and a memory of MI. Only the hypothesis of such a "Hierarchie von Gedächtnisstufen, deren höchster Gipfel unsere vom Intellekt verarbeitete Vorstellungswelt bildet, und deren erster Anfang in dem unerforschten Grenzbereiche elementarer Vorgänge liegt, in den sich Psychologie und Physiologie teilen" seems to furnish a satisfactory explanation of such well-known facts as the approximate constancy of colors and the approximate constancy of size of "Sehdinge." To endorse

this view the Marburg investigators often refer to Ewald Hering.[25]

Now the results of Krellenberg's investigation (*cf.* 66, pp. 116-119) about "Einheitsfälle" (unitary cases) who have neither AI, AB or MI but only an undifferentiated AB—that implies *e.g.*, that the AB never has the complementary color—explain why our perceptions have the above-mentioned constancy and "rationality." MI are, as a matter of course, of "rational" nature, AB show "approximately" the same structure as the MI, and these AB are the ontogenetic source of our perceptions (the Marburg investigations try to verify that for Eidetiker, and Non-Eidetiker had possibly—eidetic ancestors), ergo: the "invariance" of our perceptions is explained.

4. Upon the basis of W. Jaensch's[26] studies it is claimed that the Eidetiker differ somatically. The AB is accounted one among many psychic and somatic stigmata of the person. The differences between W. Jaensch's T-type (referring to tetany), B-type (referring to the Basedow syndrom) and BT-type as well as the differences between the AB of these types (AB_T and AB_B) cannot be described here. Perhaps the core of the very elaborate theory is that the AB_T have the characteristics of pronounced AI while in the case of the B- and BT-type we have to do with "sinnlich gesehene Vorstellungen." By

---

[25]Hering, E. *Über das Gedächtnis als eine allgemeine Funktion der organischen Materie.* Ostwald's "Klassiker der exakten Naturwissenschaften", 148.

[26]See especially op. cit. and *Ueber psychophysische Konstitutionstypen.* Münch. med. Woch., 1921, *68. Ueber psychophysische Konstitutionstypen.* Münch. med. Woch., 1922, *69.*

means of introducing calcium lacticum into the organism it is possible to split up the unitary cases of the BT-type into a Basedowoid component (AB_B) and a tetanoid component (AI and AB_T). It is stated that even *weak* AB_B are never influenced by calcium. It might be mentioned that the "pure B-type" has no complementary AB at all. AB_B are easily affected by "thinking" while AB_T show a certain independence. In the case of AB_B the person is able, *e.g.,* to influence the localization and the form of the AB to a great extent. He also has a certain influence upon the way his AB appear and disappear. We have referred to these somatic studies since they throw light upon E. R. Jaensch's method. The apsychonomic cases, *e.g.,* those of Urbantschitsch which do not ordinarily lend themselves to experimental procedure are strong B-types. In other words, a technique is provided for obtaining a "true scientific" classification of the S. On the other hand we are advised in approaching from the psychological standpoint the study of the "ordinary behavior" of AB to neglect for the present the pure B-type with its extraordinary lability of all its phenomena. (But since investigations in different localities show that the "ordinary behavior" sometimes is the behavior of the B-type we may ask whether one is justified in refusing to investigate AB from the psychological standpoint "for the present"?)

It was necessary to bring out these four points— *struktur* analytical demonstration; only "quantitatively different" laws for eidetic phenomena; hierarchy of memory-grades; and somatic basis—to show at least the general tendencies of the Marburg school. They do not, however, seem to us necessary for the investigation of AB.

It might be added that Jaensch believes the results yielded by investigations of Eidetiker are not only important for fundamental psychological questions but also for certain problems of biology, sociology, history, mythology, philology, education, and art.[27]

Our brief survey would not be complete unless we take into account the work before 1907 or 1917. Jaensch's merit is, of course, to have attacked the field of visual AB systematically. It has also been discovered that there are eidetic phenomena in other sense-fields as well.[28]   Since there have always been persons gifted in this manner, it would be strange, indeed, if eidetic phenomena had not been observed before Urbantschitsch and Jaensch. The literature gives a number of self-descriptions. Thus O. Kroh points out that certain German poets (as Otto Ludwig, Goethe, Ludwig Tieck, E. T. Hoffmann, J. V. Scheffel) were probably Eidetiker. Purkinje's book "Das Sehen in subjektiver Hinsicht" (1819)

---

[27]In this connection see especially:

Jaensch, E. R.: *Die Völkerkunde und der eidetische Tatsachenkreis.* Zsch. f. Psychol., 1922, *91*, 88.

Jaensch, E. R.: *Beziehungen von Erlebnisanalyse und Sprachwissenschaft, erläutert an den Verben der sinnlichen Wahrnehmung.* Zsch. f. Psychol. 1923, *91*, 343.

Jaensch, E. R.: *Wahrnehmungslehre und Biologie.* Zsch. f. Psychol., 1923, *93*, 129.

[28]Henning, H.: *Starre eidetische Klang- und Schmerzbilder und die eidetische Konstellation.* Zsch. f. Psychol., 1923, *92*, 137.

Compare C. C. Dimmick: *The auditory memory afterimage.* Amer. J. Psychol., 1923, *34*, 1.

seems to contain the first scientific description of visual AB. One understands why especially anatomists, physiologists and biologists are expected to possess AB. Very extensive statements can be found in Johannes Müller,[29] Henle,[30] and G. H. Meyer.[31] Meyer's observations, especially, are often referred to.[32] By means of systematic exercises Meyer got the ability "subjektive Gesichtsempfindungen willkürlich zu erwecken". In most cases these phenomena were followed by after-images. Stumpf considers L. Staudenmaier[33] on the same quest as Meyer since he worked out a scheme for evoking hallucinations in *all* sensory fields. Of great value is Fechner's attempt to establish a hierarchy of his cases "nach dem aufsteigenden Grade der Annäherung an sinnliche Phänomene." (See op. cit. chapter 44. For Fechner's own distinction between "after-images" and "imagination-images" see James op. cit. II, p. 51, between "after-images" and "memory-after-images" see James op. cit. I, p. 645.)

It goes without saying that material concerning eidetic phenomena may be found in the literature about hallu-

---

[29]Müller, J.: *Ueber die phantastischen Gesichtserscheinungen.* 1826.

[30]Henle: *Ueber das Gedächtnis in den Sinnen.* Caspars med. Wochenschrift, 1838.

[31]Meyer, G. H.: *Physiologie der Nervenfaser,* 1843.

[32]See especially James, W.: *The principles of psychology,* II, p. 66.
Fechner: *Elemente der Psychophysik,* II, p. 484.
Stumpf; op. cit., p. 75.

[33]Staudenmaier, L.: *Die Magie als experimentelle Naturwissenschaft,* 1916.

cinations and pseudohallucinations.   Some older works[34]
are of value.   G. E. Müller's discussion in his work of
1917 (op. cit. II, Teil, p. 410) also has its bearing on
our problem.   Since Anhalonium Lewinii· (peyote)
when ingested by normal adults is supposed to cause AB
the statements of certain observers[35] are of interest.

Many investigators in the field of experimental psychology came, of course, in contact with persons with AB.
One must refer to the work on visual imagery and on the
difference between "impressions" and "ideas" to apply
Hume's terms.   Especially the studies of Külpe,[36]

[34]Hibbert, S.: *Sketches of the philosophy of appari-
tions,* 1825.
Galton: *Inquiries into human faculty and its develop-
ment,* 1883.
Kandinsky: *Kritische und klinische Betrachtungen im
Gebiete der Sinnestäuschungen,* 1885.
Parish, E.: *Hallucinations and illusions, a study of the
fallacies of perception,* 1897.
[35]Ellis, H.: *Mescal, a study of a divine plant.*   Pop.
Science Monthly, 1902, *61,* 52.
Guttmann, A.: *Experimentelle Halluzinationen durch
Anhalonium Lewini.*   Schumann: Bericht über den VI.
Kongress für exp. Psych. 1914.
Fernberger, S. W.: *Observations on taking peyote.*
(Anhalonium Lewinii).   Am. J. Psychol. 1923, *34, 267,*
616.
Newberne, R. E. L. and Burke, C. H.: *Peyote.* Chilocco, Oklahoma, 1923.
[36]Külpe, O.   *Ueber die Objektivierung und Subjektivierung von Sinneseindrücken..* Phil. Studien, 1902, *18,*
508.
Also Rieffert, J.   *Ueber die Objektivierung und Subjektivierung von Sinneseindrücken.*   Schumann: Bericht
über d. V.   Kongr. f. exp. Psych. 1912.

Perky,[37] and Seashore[38] are to be mentioned in this connection. One may compare Külpe's report about Warren (op. cit. p. 526) with Warren's own statements (op. cit pp. 455-57). Special attention might be paid to the "Literaturzusammenstellung" of Anna Berliner. (Arch. f. d. ges. Psychol., 1914, *32*, 115). An examination of Lillien J. Martin's publications[39] seems to show that among her subjects were some persons gifted with AB. The "cerebral after-images" of B. Bocci[40] which are discussed by P. Busse (op. cit. p. 6) are evidently not physiological after-images. It would be instructive to learn whether in cases like Stratton's[41] eidetic phenomena played a role.

Our short survey of previous studies has brought out the fact that there exist many connections between eidetic investigations and other well worked fields in psychology. On the other hand, it is made clear that a whole group of phenomena had not been attacked up to the time of the Marburg school.

---

[37]Perky, C. W. *An experimental study of imagination.* Am. J. Psychol., 1910, *21*, 422.

[38]Seashore, C. E. *Measurements of illusions and hallucinations in normal life.* Studies fr. the Yale Psych. Lab., New Haven, 1895, III.

[39]Martin, L. J. *Die Projektionsmethode und die Lokalisation visueller und anderer Vorstellungsbilder.* Zsch. f. Psychol., 1912, *61*, 321. See her contributions in J. E. Coover: *Experiments in psychical research, 1917.*

[40]Bocci, B. *L'immagine visiva cerebrale. Contributo all' ottico fisiologica.* Roma, 1897.

[41]Stratton, G. M. *The mnemonic feat of the "Shass Pollak."* Psychol. Rev., 1917, *24*, 244.

2. SCOPE OF THE PRESENT INVESTIGATION. METHOD OF SELECTING SUBJECTS.

One might ask whether after Jaensch's elaborate research a new investigation is desirable. The necessity of new eidetic investigations has been stressed very often recently. Warren considers the AB "a promising field for research." O. Klemm (Arch. f. d. ges. Psychol., 1924, *47, 223,*) stating that the discovery of the eidetic disposition is of prime importance among "the true advances of psychology in the last decade" means that the next step has to be "diese ganze für die Jugendpsychologie entscheidende Angelegenheit auf immer breitere erfahrungsmässige Grundlagen zu stellen." Again and again Jaensch himself expresses the same view. However thorough his investigations, he was confined to limited material.

Convinced of the need of an investigation outside of Marburg—and starting from methodological presuppositions which are not quite in agreement with those of the Marburg school— I undertook the following study.

Before entering into a description of the experiments, four general principles which directed my work might be discussed.

1. One chief aim of my investigation was to collect further data on eidetic phenomena. In the present state of experimentation it is advisable to proceed in the following way: (a) to material similar to that of Jaensch (i. e. presenting almost no "pure" B-types) entirely *new* methods may be applied; (b) to material reacting quite differently from that of Marburg Jaensch's methods (or some of Jaensch's methods) may be applied. We therefore prepared a set of experiments to meet either situation.

2. Starting from the presupposition that eidetic investigations might solve certain problems of general psychology our question was: does Jaensch's interpretation seem to be adequate for the data found? Since the examination of his publications raised a certain skepticism concerning this interpretation a set of experiments was devised to test the validity of some of Jaensch's points.

3. Not much stress has been laid on the question of the frequency of the eidetic gift in any given group. In this stage of eidetic investigation qualitative studies are necessary. Until the nature of AB has been clearly defined one cannot expect to throw much light upon eidetic phenomena by means of group-investigations. I therefore tried to approach the individual case "concentrically" using as many different tests as possible. It is, moreover, highly desirable to become thoroughly acquainted with the individual in question since in many cases AB stand in an intimate relation to the emotional life of the person. (One may compare H. Henning's statement that some individuals do not get AB while experiments are performed on them since these experiments suppress the "eidetic attitude.")

4. AB meant at the outset of this investigation nothing but a "heuristic term." *Jaensch's researches suggested the general field of observation* but to work with his definition of AB would imply acceptance of his theory of the hierarchy of memory grades, a theory —and this is an important point— which is *directing* his experimental work. My intention, therefore, was on the one hand to study unusual *after*-sensations but expecting at the same time that certain *"spontaneous* phenomena" would also have to be dealt with. One has to take into consideration that the

physiological AI are by no means thoroughly and from every point of view investigated in spite of the fact that the history of investigations of this nature is comparatively long. This study, however, endeavors to bring out some characteristics, which, on the basis of our pressent knowledge, would not be ascribed to AI. S with—what might be called—"ordinary behavior" of AI have not been of interest for us since responses from such cases would contribute but little to the questions we have raised.

A total of 27 subjects were used in this investigation: 15 adult and 12 children. The group of adults consisted of 7 men and 8 women, students in Stanford University and State Teachers' College, San Jose, California. The children—6 boys and 6 girls—were pupils of grade 6A in a Palo Alto grammar school. (Except Sel.) The following table contains designation and age of the S.

	Male Subjects			Female Subjects	
	Desigation	Age		Desigation	Age
1.	Zeh	23.5	1.	Ton	19
2.	Gil	26.5	2.	Bec	19.5
3.	Wel	22	3.	Ber	23.5
4.	Mar	21.5	4.	Dem	21
5.	Wen	23	5.	Rin	17
6.	Suh	21	6.	Seh	38
7.	Ret	23	7.	Kas	20
8.	Jus	11	8.	Lin	19
9.	Col	11	9.	Laj	11.5
10.	Fow	12	10.	Sel	15
11.	Low	12	11.	Sut	12.5
12.	Nit	12	12.	Maq	13
13.	Mac	11	13.	Gil	12
			14.	Nak	11

Two points need a special explanation:

1. The reason why not more than 27 subjects are used is that qualitative studies are at present more necessary than quantitative work with groups of individuals.

2. It might be asked why adults are used while the object of the experiments is after all the "eidetic youthtype?" (a) Although I can confirm Jaensch's arguments concerning youthful observers in this field of experimentation, it is necessary to check the statements of children. (b) For the present the eidetic endowment of adults might be traced back to the persistence of a juvenile trait. There seem to be no *fundamental* differences between the eidetic phenomena of adults and children. One is therefore justified in treating the results as a whole.

A few words must be said about the group investigations by means of which the Eidetiker were found. Jaensch does not describe in detail special methods for picking out these individuals. (But compare the more recent report 46). Attention was paid to pupils with AI of long duration. Sometimes the appearance of the eyes was decisive in roughly distinguishing B-types and non-B-types.

In the group investigation of adults after a few preliminary remarks about vivid visual images, a questionnaire (see page 92) was presented. Then a few short experiments were performed: (1) Before the class a red square (10 x 10 cm.) on a neutral gray background was exposed for 40 sec. After the removal of the square the members of the class fixated a mark which had been covered by the square during the exposure. The E called the time every 10 sec. The students, when the image had completely disappeared, had to write down the time of duration of their AI and observations concerning their appearance. (2) The experiment was repeated with an exposure of *10* sec. (3) and (4), A silhouette of a human head cut out of black cardboard was used. The times of exposure were 10 and 40 sec., respectively.

The presence of AB might be expected in some instances where the questionnaires showed many "yes" answers and long durations of AI. The S here reported on are taken from this group.

DATA ON SOME CHARACTERISTICS OF VISUAL IMAGERY

Name ....

Address ....

I—1. Can you get very vivid and clear visual images if you wish?........
   2. Can you get very vivid visual images of faces which are well known to you?........
   3. Can you "see" (imagine with the vividness of a perception) objects you like or often use?......
   4. Do you sometimes have vivid visual images in twilight?........
   5. Do you sometimes have vivid visual images when you are excited?........
   6. Having finished some reading in a text-book can you visually recall the pages?........
   7. Can you clearly see the headings and paragraph divisions used in the text?........
   8. Can you see the *exact* location of every word as in a photograph?........

9. After memorizing a printed passage do you call up a visual image of the passage and read it as if it were reality?........

10. Have you ever had this ability?........
   If so, when?........

11. Do you make use of visual images in describing objects which are not present? (Pictures, etc.)........

12. Do you make use of visual images in geometry? ....

13. Looking fixedly at an object, did it ever happen that this object seemed to change its form?......

14. Do you know of any individual who has unusually vivid visual images?......Adult.....Child.....
   Please give his name and address on the other side of the sheet.

II.   Experiment   I   Time ....   Quality ....
               II   ....
              III   ....
              IV   ....

The following table illustrates these group-investigations:

	Number of cases	Number of cases where the questionnaire seems to indicate the presence of AB	No. of cases[1] where our experimental methods probably would have discovered AB
Stanford	212	20	10 — 13
San Jose	154	64	32 — 43
	366	84	42 — 56

[1]Because of external, etc. reasons, it was not possible

It might be noticed: (1) that the College in San Jose is attended almost exclusively by women; (2) that 23 individuals out of 366 gave name and address of other persons with "unusually vivid visual images." If the intention is only to find Eidetiker to be tested our method of selection seems quite satisfactory. Individual examination of some questionnaires, however, proved that some questions gave rise to misunderstandings since they were not simple enough. On the other hand the relatively high number of questions for a brief investigation of this sort and the varied character of these questions were compensating factors. At all events the test served to furnish a group of subjects suitable to work with.

In a class of 32 pupils (grade VIA of the public school, Channing Ave., Palo Alto) 12 children with AB were taken. Undoubtedly the number would have been higher if we had intended a determination of the percentage of Eidetiker. In the group investigation with children no use was made of the questionnaire. Only the experiments above mentioned were performed. Questions raised by the children were answered by the E. The great interest these boys and girls of 11-12 years showed was startling.

In general, our experience with the group-investigations brought out the fact that an investigator working in the above mentioned localities would apparently have no difficulty in obtaining adequate subjects of both sexes, either children or adults.

---

in every instance to follow up certain cases, but our experience with our material has led us to conclude that in the above mentioned numbers we should have found evidence of AB.

3. DESCRIPTION AND DATA OF THE EXPERIMENTS

The order in which the experiments are described is for convenience determined by the kind of stimulus material used. At the same time I shall try to make clear what viewpoints determined this choice of material. It must be noticed that not all experiments have been performed on the whole group of 27 subjects. There are two reasons: (1) These experiments demand considerable time from the individual subject. In spite of the great interest most of the reagents showed, there is naturally a certain limit so far as time is concerned. (2) Certain experiments—and this is the main point—can only be performed on "strong" cases. It is not possible e. g. to investigate the "Kovariantenphänomen" ("phenomena of covariants") with persons who have faint AB. In fact, E. R. and W. Jaensch (op. cit.) distinguish five stages of the "eidetic attitude" each stage indicating a certain "degree" of this aptitude. Jaensch's method of using certain S to test some special points was therefore adopted.

The experimental work was carried on in 1924, and most of it was done in the Psychological Laboratory of Stanford University. Some cases were investigated in Palo Alto and San Jose.

The S was seated at the narrow end of a table. The table, 0.75 m. x 2.43 m. and 0.71 m. high, was of a muddy yellow-brown color and so placed that the daylight came from the left, passing between the eyes of the S and a background standing on the table. In no instance was artificial light used. (In some cases the arrangement was different as indicated below.)   In the beginning of the experiments the background *always* was placed at a distance of 0.5 m from the S.   This background—Hering's gray paper 30, 35 x 38 cm., with a a black frame of about 2 cm. width—could be tilted forwards and backwards from the vertical position in which it was usually placed.   In the experiments with measurements the background always was placed in such a position that the square to be measured was on a level with the eyes during the exposure.   In the case of children no head-rest was used.   The pupils were instructed to lean the head against an iron rod covered with cloth.   Having obtained thus quite a convenient position of the head the background could be placed at the distance wanted.[1]

1. EXPERIMENTS WITH GEOMETRIC FIGURES

A. *Size and color—at distances different from the distance of exposure (heterodiastatic constellations.)*

Squares of 5 cm. dimensions (see page 154, figure 17) were used unless otherwise noted.   The colored papers made by Milton Bradley Company were pasted on pieces of cardboard having the size just indicated.   The following nine colors were taken: 1. red, 2. orange red, 3. orange, 4. yellow, 5. green, 6. blue, 7. violet (shade No. 1), 8. black, and 9. white..   (In their reports the S called 2 red, and 3 purple.)   Beside the Milton Bradley papers use

[1]Compare H. Henning's fear that the eidetic experiment might be an "Isolierschemel" in op. cit. 24, p. 143.

Also: *Neue Typen der Vorstellungsbilder and die Entwicklung des Vorstellens.*   Zsch. f. angew. Psychol., 1923, *22,* 387.

was made of Hering's gray No. 30. A thin black thread
attached to an eyelet on the backside of each square
made it possible to expose the square on a level with
the eyes and without the hands of the experimenter be-
coming distracting stimuli. In case measurements were
taken the color-square was pasted in the centre of the
gray background. This square used for measurements
was either red (red orange) or yellow. (Koffka: "Ein
Einfluss der Farbe auf die Grösse ist bisher noch nicht
festgestellt worden."[2]) In one series of experiments the
time of exposure was 10 sec., in another series 40 sec.
In the former series after the end of the exposure the
square *with* the background was removed, thus exposing
a second background of exactly the same size and quality.
On this background the S saw the image (I) either at
once or after some moments. (To avoid committing myself on the question whether we have to do with an AB
or an AI we use this indifferent term I.) Then the
background was placed at a distance of 100 cm. After
having measured the I-square the background was placed
at 150 cm., hereafter at 25 cm. Measurements also were
taken at these distances. In the second series, 40 sec.
exposure, the square was measured only at a distance
of 100 and 150 cm. In both series the size of the square
was not determined in the isodiastatic constellation (distance of I = distance of original stimulus, here 50 cm.)
to adopt Koffka's term. The measurement of the second
series (after 40 sec. exposure) have never been taken
on the same days, but always three or more days later.
The instruction in the 40 sec. series was to fixate the

---

[2]Koffka, K. *Ueber die Messung der Grösse von Nachbildern.* Psychol. Forsch., 1923, *3, 219.*

square. In the 10 sec. experiment the S was asked merely to "look at the square" and to try afterwards to see it again. The compass used to determine the size of the squares was made of aluminum, its feet having a length of about 11 cm. The compass was adjusted to a size greater than the expected I, one of its feet was then moved forwards to the lower side of the I. The S was to tell exactly when the foot touches this side. Then the other foot was similarly applied to the upper side. The measurements therefore were "vertical measurements from the outside." The size was determined only when the square showed *sharp contours*. The results of these measurements are embodied in the table on page 101, each value representing the vertical distance between the upper and the lower side of the most *distinct square* the S could get. The measurements of AB which Paula Busse (5) obtained from her 8 S at the distances of 100, 150 and 25 cm. are also included for comparison (p. 102). The table on page 102 (27 S) contains observations concerning the appearance of AB: time of exposure 10 sec. unless otherwise noted. In this connection it must be mentioned that during the whole experimental work, emphasis was laid upon gathering *spontaneous* remarks of the S since in many cases eidetic phenomena stand in an intimate relation with the "inner life" of the person.

With regard to these experiments some general points must be emphasized. As will be noticed we were not concerned with the measurements of MI. There are several reasons:

1. It is hardly advisable to investigate the difficult problem of the projection of MI coincidently with eidetic studies. If one recalls the intricacy of this problem as

presented by G. E. Müller (op. cit. II, p. 76. Ueber die Beziehung zwischen Entfernung und Grösse bei egozentrisch lokalisierten Vorstellungsbildern) one can only conclude that *special* investigations will help to overcome the difficulties.

2. No effort was made here to prove that the AB occupy a central position in a continuum of "Gedächtnisstufen."

3. It is hardly advisable to take a compass in order to measure a phenomenon that cannot be seen, at least not in the sense AB and AI can be seen. Moreover, one has not to forget that some of the S were children.

Therefore we have been interested only in those phenomena Jaensch calls AB and AI. How is it possible to distinguish them? The E naturally has first to know the differences of the *conditions* under which they arise. Jaensch and his co-workers consider three points to be important:

(1) *the time of exposure* (see on the one hand Busse, Gösser, Gottheil, on the other hand Krellenberg),

(2) *the mode of fixation* (whether staring at a point or with eyes wandering),

(3) *the intention* of the observer to see something. (The intention to see the object is, however, not always a pre-requirement.)

In our experiments we used the exposure-time of Gösser for AB: 10 sec., and for the production of AI: 40 sec. (P. Busse). Corresponding to these different exposure-times different modes of fixation were used: with 10 sec. exposure the S were allowed to look at it "as they liked," with 40 sec. steady fixation was demanded.

There is no doubt that time is one of the most important factors influencing AB as well as AI. The next step after Jaensch's work would have been, therefore, a systematic study of this factor. Thus one may vary the time keeping the modes of fixation constant and vice versa. We decided not to attempt this but to start from Jaensch's results which claim a sharp difference between AI and AB. *What happens if one takes the time and the mode of fixation suggested there?* It may be remarked that in many cases 10 sec. are not necessary to get an AB. The S after a few seconds often looks bored and is impatient with the remainder of the exposure. But the above mentioned exposure-times are used to create a comparative basis. In our 10 sec. experiments the S was asked to *try* to see the stimulus material again. Even when not given this instruction many S spontaneously fall into this attitude. A discussion of the questionnaire between E and S which preceded the experiments caused in many cases such an attitude towards the material presented. Under *these* circumstances the instruction of the E did nothing but state explicitly what in fact was "in the mind" of many reagents. At the same time it was, of course, also given to those who would have had an AB without consciously trying to. By such means a comparative basis was created.[3]

As above stated in series I the measurements were taken at the distances 100, 150, and 25 cm. The *same* I was measured. The same method was applied in series II. The Marburg reports are not clear about this point. Only Gottheil (21), in investigating the AI of adults, states that the size of the square could only very seldom be measured in more than one position of the background.

---

[3]The S were not asked to close the eyes as in 100.

Our method implies that the I had to last at least 2 minutes.

Gösser's law concerning the degree of plasticity of AI, AB and MI furnishes the justification for the Marburg investigators to adopt a certain order for the measurements: (1) MI, (2) AB, (3) AI. In our experiments 2 and 3 are separated by an interval of several days. Some occasional measurements indicated (a) that there was often a difference between the length of the horizontal and the length of the vertical side, (b) that the values obtained by a "measurement from the outside" differed from the values obtained by approaching the boundaries from the inside. For our purpose, however, the vertical measurement from the outside seemed to be sufficient. (See below.)

A. *Size and color—at distances different from the distance of exposure (heterodiastatic constellations.)*

A1. *Size after*

Subject	10 sec. exposure			40 sec. exposure	
	100 cm.	150 cm.	25 cm.	100 cm.	150 cm.
a. Zeh	6	6.2	10.5	10	15
Laj	4	5.5	8	6.6	6.6
Lil	3.5	3	6.5	9.5	14
Sel	5	4	6.4	6	4.8
Mar	4.6	3.6	5.4	8.9	12.1
Maq	7	10.5	6.5	9.1	11
b. Wel	5.2	5.4	9	8.5	11
Rin	5	5.1	6.7	10	15
Sut	5.5	5.5	7	10	15
Ret	6.4	5.8	7	11.5	14
Seh	4.5	4.6	12.5	6.1	8
Kas	5	5.5	4.6	9	12.5

Jus	6.4	11.8	5	8.6	14
Wen	5.8	9.7	8	9	11
Suh	3	4.3	25.2	10	15
Col	12.4	16.5	3.7	11.4	15.4
Gil	6.5	7	13.2	13.5	6.5
Ton	9.5	14	3.1	10	15
Fow				10	15
Bec				10	15
Ber				10	15
Low					
Dem					
Lin					
Nit					
Nak					
Mac					

Size after 15 sec. exposure in Paula Busse's table.

(5, p. 42)

Names of S	100 cm.	150 cm.	25 cm.
Heinrich F.	9.6	14.1	1.4
Fritz U.	11.0	15.8	3.8
Paul B.	5.0	4.7	4.7
Georg W.	10.5	16.2	1.4
Werner P.	12.5	15.4	4.4
Erwin Mr.	10.5	16.4	4.2
Philipp B.	10.9	18.7	3.0
Guntram S.	10.6	14.3	5.3

A2

Subject	Exposure-time.	Color of stimulus	Appearances observed
Zeh	10″	red	light reddish square, becomes dimmer and darker gradually, stays to the place.
Lil	10″	red	red square, "does not go with the eyes, seems to stay pretty close to the place."
Wel	10″	yellow	yellow square 7 sec., then dark intermittently.

Wel	10″	yellow	yellow square 4 sec., then dark intermittently.
Mar	10″	red	red persistently, "more tangible than the green" of AI.
Wen	10″	yellow	yellow with yellow halo 10 sec., then blue with yellow halo persistently.
Wen	10″	orange	"the same shade and size" 10 sec., then bluish.
Suh	10″	yellow	blue, "seems original size," finally dark in the center, surrounded by blue.
Ret	10″	yellow	light color ("between yellow and white"), then purple.
Ret	10″	yellow	yellowish, then purple.
Ret	10″	green	green, dark red, then "light color."
Jus	10′	red	"black" and red alternately.
Col	10″	red	green intermittently.
Fow	10″	red	"green, has the same size," becomes smaller, then dark.
Low	10″	red	green 1 min., then purple, then yellow and white, etc.
Nit	10″	red	green and red alternately.
Mac	10″	violet	yellow intermittently.
Ton	10″	yellow	distinct yellow 3 sec., then blue.
Ton	10″	yellow	1. yellow "much bigger than natural size." 2. blue square with yellow halo.
Ton	10″	yellow	big yellow circle, tnen blue square, in the original size.
Bec	10″	red	pink, becomes dimmer and fades away.
Bec	10″	red	red persistently.
Bec	10″	yellow	purple, yellow glow around it.
Ber	10″	red	S gets nothing.

Ber	30″	red	green persistently.
Dem	10″	red	red, but "a green light covers the whole thing."
Rin	10″	blue	yellow persistently.
Rin	3″	blue	blue persistently.
Seh	10″	red	gray persistently.
Seh	10″	red	greenish gray persistently.
Kas	10″	blue	yellow persistently, sometimes somewhat brighter.
Lin	10″	red	green persistently.
Laj	10″	red	red persistently.
Laj	10″	red	green with red spot in the center.
Laj	5″	red	square "without color."
Sel	10″	yellow	yellow persistently.
Sel	5″	yellow	yellow persistently.
Sut	10″	red	red 4 sec., then dark.
Maq	10″	red	green, then red persistently.
Maq	10″	blue	yellow and blue alternately.
Maq	10″	yellow	blue and yellow alternately.
Gil	10″	red	red, green, then black.
Gil	10″	yellow	yellow 4 sec., then purple, then black.
Gil	10″	red	red, then green surrounded with red.
Nak	10″	red	"green the same size," becomes smaller, finally grayish.

B. *Size—studied at a distance equal to the distance of exposure (isodiastatic constellation),*

(exposure time 10 sec.)

Since after the removal of the square exposed some S spontaneously remarked: "It is bigger now" or "It is smaller" a group of seven individuals was selected to determine the size in the isodiastatic consellation. There are further reasons why measurements were desirable. The 50 cm.—column of P. Busse (5, p. 42) showed some rather large deviations from the expected size of 5 cm. (6. 1; 6. 3; 6. 4 cm.) Jaensch on the basis of a much larger material explained this deviation by a T_E (epileptotetanoid) constitution which is supposed to be inclined toward macroscopy. According to him Busse's material consisted of pure B-types and T_E — types.[4]

Column A of our table gives values immediately obtained after the removal of the 5 cm.-square.

Column B: Values obtained after the square has been measured at the distances of 100, 150, and 25 cm. (Vertical measurement from the outside.)

B. Size—studied at a distance equal to the distance of exposed (isodiastatic constellation).

Subject	A		B	
Lil	4.6	5.1	6.5	7.1
Wel	3.5	6	5.1	8.0
Mar	4.4	4.7	5.2	5.3
Laj	5.5	7.9	4	3.0
Ret	3.5	4.0	5.3	4.9
Rin	5	5.1	5.2	5.3
Zeh	7	8	8.3	11.1

C. Size—studied at a distance equal to the distance of exposure, the background being a picture

The gray background was replaced by a colored picture. The red square (10 x 10 cm.) standing before this picture covered a considerable part of the lower half of the picture. First the vertical, after that the horizontal distance was determined. The measurements for 9

---

[4]Jaensch, E. R., *Zur Richtigstellung und Ergänzung.* Zsch. f. Psychol., 1922, *88,* 317.

S are contained in the table on this page. In addition to this further observations concerning certain S are included.

Some questions brought forth in experiments of this nature are: What happens if the homogeneous gray background is replaced by an inhomogeneous multi-colored background? Are there no difficulties to see the AB in spite of the "distracting" background? Is the final outcome of the "competition" that the background disappears or that the AB disappears? Do the AB and the background mix? P. Busse was interested in the determination of the "weight" of AI, AB and MI. (See op. cit. p. 27). Our question was: What is the size of the AB *if* an AB with distinct contours can be seen?

C. *Size—studied at a distance equal to the distance of exposure, the background being a picture.*

Subject	Vertical distance	Horizontal distance
Rin	9	8
Suh	8.9	8.9
Zeh	9.2	9
Mar	8.3	8.1
Kas	7.8	7.4
Wel	8.5	8
Laj	7.7	7.7
Lil	9	8.6
Ret	9.9	8.9

S Kas, Wel and Ret see "a greenish square" the other subjects have positive AB.

Suh a. 10 sec. S sees "a colorless square" on the picture.

b. 20 sec.—10 min., but could see it indefinitely. (E turns the picture so that it stands on its left side.)
S sees "a bright light square. It is not red."
(The picture in different positions: lying before

the S the left vertical side near to the S; the upper side near to the S; standing again, but upside down. S remarks): "It is always the same size."

(E measures the square on the picture standing upside down: 7.8 x 7.8): "It seems to be the original size." (E removes the picture.) "Now it is red." (E measures the square on the gray background: 7.8 x 7.8). (E turns the background 45° to the right): Vertical dist. 8 cm. horizontal dist. 7 cm. (Then the background in the former position.)

Distance	2 m.—	Vert. dist. 8 cm.,		horiz. dist. 7.8 cm.			
"	0.5 m.—	"	" 7.6	"	"	" 6.7	"
"	0.5 m.—	"	" 7.8	"	"	" 7.6	"

(white background)

white background lying		"	" 8.2	"	"	" 6.7	"

before S

S thinks the square is always the same size.

Dem   10 sec. S sees the red square on the picture. "I can see the picture through the square. The red is lying on it." Suddenly the square turns 45° to the right. (S is surprised).

Rin   10 sec. S sees the red on the picture.

Vert. dist. 9 cm.	Horiz. dist. 8 cm.	(50 cm. dist.)					
"	" 5.5	"	"	" 6.2	"	(100 " ")	

(E removes the picture)

"	" 4.9	"	"	" 5.1	"	(200 " ")	
"	" 9.1	"	"	" 8.5	"	(50 " again.)	

D. *Form—the background tilted 45° to the right.*

(Exposure time 10 sec.)

Experiments of this kind were expected to throw light upon the relation of the AB to the background and upon the factors influencing the form and size. It must be remembered that Busse's results with the ellipse (see loc. cit. p. 21) were used to support the law of invariance. A group of 8 individuals was taken in our experiments. The 5. cm. square was red; it was exposed at 50 cm. distance.

D. *Form—the background tilted 45° to the right*

1. Laj. a. "Almost a line." (Vertical)

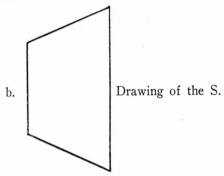

b.   Drawing of the S.

2. Sel. a. "It's a real square." (5.5×5.5)[5]
   b. "It seems to be the same." (5.4×5.3)
3. Ret. a. "A square." (7×4.5)
   b. "A square." (6.4×4.5)

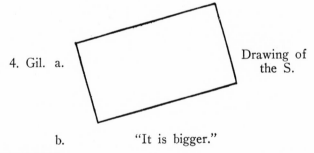

4. Gil. a.   Drawing of the S.

b.   "It is bigger."

_____

[5]The first number always indicates the vertical distance.

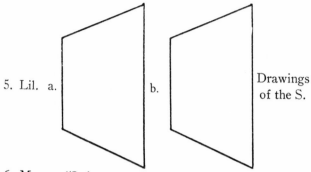

5. Lil. a.   b.   Drawings of the S.

6. Mac. a. "It becomes almost a line."
     b. "The line is a little bit wider."
7. Nit. a. "A line is standing there."

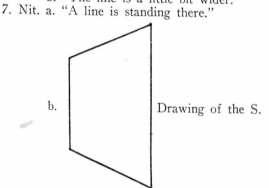

b.   Drawing of the S.

8. Rin. a. }
     b. } "It is standing in the air. The position has not changed."

Ret and Mac sees a greenish AB, the others a red one.

E. *Mixtures of various geometric figures.*

For studying color-mixtures in the AB, one has to have persons who seeing stimultaneously two or more AB (which are, of course, spatially separated) are able to project one AB on the other. Jaensch found S who mixed the AB with real objects; e.g. a blue *AB* was projected on a yellow *objective* square of the same size. Stumpf (op. cit. p. 107) knows only *one* case in the former literature which is, however, open to objections: *Gruber* gives an account of a Roumanian scholar and poet who mixed a yellow photism caused by the word "doî" with an objective red. The result was orange. As above stated, the Marburg investigators were interested in the mixture of the colors of AB with objective colors.[6] In general Gösser's observers did not succeed very well in mixing AB and "background-square," Herwig's and Jaensch's reagents, however, could mix under certain circumstances:—

(1) if the squares were "not too big;"

(2) if the AB were projected in a frame *behind* which the objective color was exposed. (In spite of Gösser's explanation op. cit. p. 119 it seems to us as if Gösser's and Herwig-Jaensch's observations are totally different.)

Performing some experiments intended to check the results of these investigators and which by the way, led to observations as reported by Gösser (op. cit. p. 117) and Herwig and Jaensch (op. cit. p. 223) we got certain cues which made us think of the possibility of mixing colored AB. Observations in this direction have value as objective results if the S knows nothing about the laws of color-mixture. Our data, pp. 111-117 refer to

[6]See Gottheil op. cit. p. 83, Gösser op. cit. p. 116 and Herwig, B. & Jaensch, E. R. *Ueber Mischung von objektiv dargebotenen Farben mit Farben des Anschauungsbildes.* Zsch. f. Psychol., 1921, *87,* 217.

three S: Rin, Dem, and Lil; but only the observations of Rin are of interest in this connection since the remarks of Dem are only reported to show a case where the *results* of color-mixture are determined to some extent by "will' and "thinking." The observations of Lil show a case where the Eidetiker is unable to produce mixture. Rin knew "nothing about the color-wheel." She remarked once after having mixed red and green: "Why do I see gray? In painting it is different." She had taken no course in psychology.

Concerning the experiments with two squares (see below) it must be remarked: 5 cm. squares were exposed for 2-3 sec., the upper edge of each square being 15 cm. distant below the upper edge of the background. The distance from one square to the other was about 10 cm. The color named first in the table (see below) is the square that was exposed first to the left. The second square was exposed immediately after the removal of the first one. The S always sees the complementary color after an exposure longer than two or three seconds. If the time is shorter than 2 or 3 seconds the original color will be seen indefinitely.

E. *Mixtures of various geometric figures*

Rin.

> I. Mixtures of *two* squares (binocular exposure). (The colors named below refer to AB. The AB named first is placed upon the second one.)

1. red-blue	"very dark color."
2. blue-red	"bluish red, very dark."
3. yellow-red	"yellowish red—a color between the two."
4. red-yellow	"dull color."

5. blue-violet ⎫
6. violet-blue ⎬ "dark purple."

7. purple-green ⎫ "not purple and not green,
8. green-purple ⎬ but between the two."

9. gray-black ⎫ "black square."
10. black-gray ⎬

11. gray-red "blackish."
12. red-gray "reddish black."
13. red-green "dark gray" ⎫ "There is very
14. green-red "dark gray" ⎬ little difference
                              in shade."

15. orange-violet "dark gray, some reddish tinge in it."
16. violet-orange "a little bit darker now."
17. yellow-blue "light green."
18. blue-yellow "darker green."
19. white-black ⎫ S brings them side by side.
20. black-white ⎬ but cannot mix them.

II. Measurements of the mixtures in 1, 3, 5, 7, 9, 11: 5.9; 6; 6.3; 6.2; 7. (Vertical distance.)

III. Between 5 and 6 the following experiments (monocular exposure) have been performed:

1. Yellow exposed to the left eye 2 sec. S sees yellow with the right eye for an indefinite time.
2. Red exposed to the right eye 2 sec. S sees red with the left eye for an indefinite time.
3. The same with orange and green, i.e. S always sees the *same* color with the eye which was closed during the exposure.
4. Yellow exposed to the left 10 sec. S sees purple with the right eye indefinitely.
5. The same with other colors: S sees the complementary color with the eye which was closed during the exposure.

IV. Between 13 and 14 some experiments without exposure have been done.

Upon the remark of the S: "Why do you expose red again? I can see it anyway if I wish." E asks to see green to the right and violet to the left.

S sees the two colors. ("Place the green on violet.") "It is greenish violet." ("Place the violet on green.") "It is a darkish green."

(This procedure was repeated with other colors. The results of the mixtures are as indicated in I.)

V. AB and objective square on the background.

1. Yellow AB and blue square.

S tries to place the yellow AB on the blue square, but does not succeed. She cannot place it *beside* the blue square; "it stays in the right lower corner of the background."

2. Blue AB and blue square.

The same: S cannot place the AB on the square.

3. Yellow AB and blue square. Distances as indicated p. 111). S tries to get a blue AB from the square and to place it on the yellow AB. *Finally* she sees the blue AB in the right lower corner, moves the yellow AB down and mixes them there. "But the blue square is still disturbing." S sees a "green square."

VI. Further data to illustrate the behavior of Rin's AB of squares.

1. Red exposed 2 sec., violet exposed 10 sec. S sees a red and yellowish AB and mixes them (yellowish red.)

2. Red exposed 10 sec., violet 2 sec.

S mixes green and violet. (greenish violet.)

3. Red and violet are simultaneously exposed for 2 sec. S sees a red and a violet AB. ("Look at the violet and place the red on it.") S tries but does not succeed.

4. Red on gray.
   S sees a reddish black square. ("Now look into the left lower corner of the background.") S does not see the AB there. "Do you want me to bring it there " S places it there.

5. Orange and violet.
   ("Can you turn the violet square 45° in such a way that it is standing on one corner?") S tries and then sees the *violet* standing in the required position. Looking at the *orange* square she finds that it also stands in this position. At this movement the violet square returns to the former position. S does not succeed in seeing both at the same time in this position. Finally she places the violet on orange.

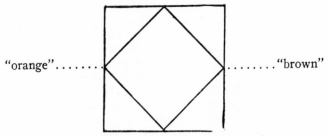

"orange"........   ...."brown"

6. S looks through a reading glass at a red square. 10 sec. (E removes reading glass and square at the same time.) S

sees a green square which has the same size as the red square previously seen through the reading glass.

7. The same, but E does not remove the reading glass. S sees a green square of the *same* size. (E removes the reading glass.) The size of the green AB does not change. (The AB is projected on the background standing 50 cm. before the S): "It is somewhat bigger now."

8. S looks through a reading glass at two squares in the following position.

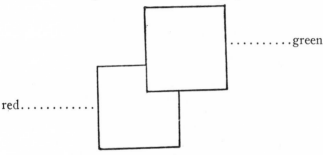

(After the removal of the squares) S sees a purple square on a greenish blue square (position as in drawing), then suddenly a red square on a green one. (The reading-glass is moved.) The AB change size.

9. Green circle (diameter 5 cm.) on red square (5 cm. on a side.) S sees a dark brownish circle and four red corners.

10. Red square (5 cm.) on green circle (5 cm.) S sees a greenish circle *in t*he red square. The circle does not touch the edges of the square.

11. Blue cube (6 cm. on a side) 2 sec. S only sees the blue front side standing in

a vertical position. S "tries" to see the whole cube, but does not succeed.

12. Blue and yellow cube (10 cm. distance) 2 sec. S sees the two front sides in the original color but cannot move them.

13. Blue and yellow cube (10 cm. distance) 10 sec. S sees the complementary colors of the front sides, but cannot mix them. (Also red and green.)

14. Gray circle (diameter, 5 cm; a sector of 30° cut out, p. 154 fig. 19) on red circle. S sees a reddish brown circle with a red sector.

15. Gray triangle (altitude 5.5 cm.) on a white square (5 cm. on a side), S sees a "black" triangle on a white square. S does not see the apex.

16. Squares of different colors are attached to the moving pendulum of a metronome. S sees—after the removal of the squares in question—an arch in the complementary color.

VII. Mixtures of *three* squares

1. Green—red—yellow.
S tries to place green on red; the yellow disappears. Now S places them together in such a way that the edges touch. ("Gradually move green on red.") S sees from the left to the right: green, dark brown, red, yellow. Then: brown with yellow tinges in it, yellow. "Almost no difference between these two colors." Finally: a yellowish square.

2. Purple—green—red. S tries to place the red on green: the purple disappears. Now S places them side by side. ("Place red on green.") S sees from the right to the left: red, reddish brown, green,

purple. Then: "A very dark square." (5.7 cm. vertical distance, 5.6 cm. horizontal distance.)

3. Yellow—red (10 cm.)—green. ("Place yellow and green on the red square.") S sees the AB as indicated in diagram:

"red"

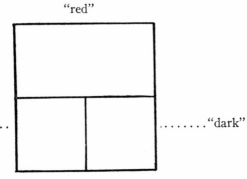

"brown"......   ...."dark"

Dem   1. Yellow—blue, 2 sec.
S sees either yellow or blue, finally she gets both at the same time. S then gradually moves the yellow over the blue and sees the *whole* yellow square and the rest of the blue square not yet covered. "But I changed it. I can see it as I want to."

2. Gray—blue, 2 sec. S sees a *black* and a blue square. She can perform every movement and change of color "at will."

Lil.   (S reports that he cannot move the AB-squares.) Red—green, 2 sec. S sees the two colors. "With great effort" S places them side by side, but does not succeed in mixing them.

F. *Mixtures by means of a stereoscope.*

Experiments with the stereoscope might be considered as "objective" tests if the following arrangements is taken: first a stereoscopic card is presented to be moved by the S until the objects on this picture. can be seen clearly and distinctly. After the removal of this slide the "test"-slide, half of which is covered by a piece of cardboard, is introduced. After the end of the exposure time the other half is likewise covered by a cardboard. The E waits until the S sees the I plainly on this cardboard. He then removes the first cardboard. The S now draws and describes what he has seen. In our experiments the exposure time was not fixed. The S could look at half of the slide as long as he wanted. The pieces of cardboard used were white. First the E tried with slides presenting simple objects and the results soon showed that it was not possible to experiment with "complicated" ones. With fourteen S the slides as shown on p. 154 fig. 16 was used, part *a* being covered during the exposure. Results could only be obtained by five persons. (See pp. 118-120.) In the case of the other nine S the AB suddenly disappeared after the removal of the first cardboard or it stayed for a short time moving around on the sheet.

F. *Mixture by means of a stereoscope.*

Drawings of the S.

Jus.

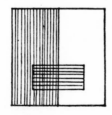

Dark oblong

Suh.

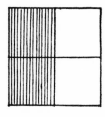

White oblong

Mar.

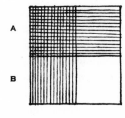

a. "entirely black."
b. "black."
c. "white."

Dem.

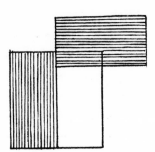

Dark oblong

Laj.

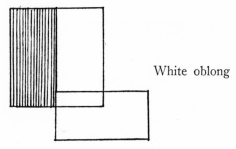

White oblong

G. *Oblong card filled with various geometric figures.*

A white cardboard (9 x 36 cm.) on which three rows of geometric forms were printed was exposed for 30 sec. Every row contained fourteen figures, the first one for instance, from left to the right: oblong, triangle, three squares, oblong, triangle, two oblongs, square, two oblongs, square, oblong. A total of twelve S were taken. Six S reported, as did Wel. The other observations are reported on p. 121. A longer exposure-time did not change the type of response.

G. *Oblong card filled with geometric figures.*
Col.

S sees three rows in black.

(Drawing of S)

Low. S sees purple, then white forms which cannot be distinguished; finally a blue.

Maq. S sees white forms for a few seconds. Forms are "almost" the original ones. The forms turn black: the first row contains nothing but triangles. S knows that it was different. "I can't help it."

Lil. S sees 7 forms—first row 3, second row 4 forms —in black. "I see the center ones, but I can imagine many of the rest." The figures are black.

Nak. S sees "a few of them for a short time" in yellow. Then they turn green.

Wel. S sees "all the forms quite plainly." Forms— white color—disappear after 4 sec.

    H. *Various forms.*

In a number of preliminary experiments some rather challenging observations were made. The data on pp. 121-122 are added to illustrate certain points concerning the behavior of the AB of the person in question. The stimulus material used with Rin. (see below) may be seen on p. 154 fig. 15. The square on the left (a) was pink, in (b) a green circle was surrounded by red. The color-wheel used with Dem. (p. 122) is the same as printed in Ch. L. Myers: Experimental Psychology, Cambridge, 1914, between p. 2 and 3.

    H. *Various forms.*

Rin. a. 15 sec.—4 min. S sees a "green circle to the left, a red circle to the right," but does not see the rest. (S is surprised.) Distance between the two circles 4. 5 cm. (Real distance 4 cm.)

    b. 15 sec. S only sees "two squares both of which are green. It is the same green. Between the circles is a white space. I do not see any spots, corners or circles." Distance between the two squares 2.9 cm. (Real distance 1.9 cm.)

Low.   Red square (5 x 5) 10 sec.—3 min. S sees "a green square. Sort of points stick out. The sides are not smooth."

(After 1 min.) : "Now it becomes smaller. It is perfectly purple." The I dissapears. " Now I see it again; it has a clear-cut yellow shape with a black outline. Now the outline is white. Oh, that is a face. I do not know why that should be." (S indicates by a drawing that he sees a dark roundish form with a white outline and a dark "cap.")

(After 4.5 min.) : "Now there is a milky white square—now it is sort of yellow—now it turns back to white again—there is the face again— he is facing me—there is no cap—it is exactly like a face."

Dem. a. 45 sec. (During the exposure S sees a blue circle around the color wheel.) S sees a yellow wheel which is blue at the one side. There is a gradual transition from one color to the other. Then the circle becomes entirely blue. The circle becomes a blue triangle. (Looking at me) : "I see the blue on you." (Looking through blue transparent paper) : "The blue turns into a deeper blue." (Looking through green glass) : "It's a kind of orange."

    b. 60 sec. (During the exposure S sees the blue contour again.) "I see the different colors quite distinctly." Then: "The one side becomes greenish blue. The other side becomes yellowish orange."

    c. 60 sec. S sees green and white wheels. Squares and circles appear and reappear.

II. *EXPERIMENTS WITH PICTURES OF ANIMALS*
(See fig. 1-10).

The value of pictures in experiments has often been pointed out. In the case of Eidetiker one might expect

Fig. 1

Fig. 2

Fig. 3

Fig. 4

Fig. 5

Fig. 6

Fig. 7

Fig. 8

Fig. 9

Fig. 10

that the I of pictures would differ in their behavior from the I of squares. In general, we have here the difference between "interesting" and "uninteresting" objects: at least for children the yellow cardboard-lion and yellow cardboard-square have a different *meaning*.

It goes without saying that every investigator of eidetic phenomena will make use of pictures. Urbantschitsch did so (97, pp. 163-211), but his records merely report: "that the subject sees the picture" or "all important things in the picture" or "all the details.'" And even Jaensch reports more general points: positive or negative AB, etc. In our experiments emphasis is laid upon getting more specific descriptions. But it will be necessary first to state at least a few of the problems involved in experiments with picture-animals by such means making clear what viewpoints have directed our observations.

In what way does the S look at the objective picture? Does he see the I at once or after an interval? Does a second exposure of the same length increase the distinctness and clearness of the I? What happens after the removal of the picture? Is there a state intermediate between "imagination" and "visualization?" Do· *all* objects which the S finally sees appear at the same time? If not, in what sequence do they appear? Why just this sequence? What does not appear at all, ahd why not? Have the objects the original color or "no color?" Do *some* of the objects have a color differing from the original ones? What is the relation of the I to the background? Do reversals of positions take place?[7]

---

[7]See e. g. Stern, W. *Ueber verlagerte Raumformen.* Zsch. f. angew. Psychol. 1909, 2.

Are they symmetrical or asymmetrical? Do these reversals take place in spite of a steady fixation? Does the S believe he caused them? Is it possible that the position of the picture during the exposure (e.g. standing or hanging) influences the behavior of the I? Does the I disappear and reappear? Is it influenced by distracting stimuli? Do questions cause the appearance of phenomena not seen up to that moment? Are the objects in the I standing in a fixed position? Do certain movements take place? Can the S cause movements 'at will?' Are eye movements involved in this shift of position? Does the I sometimes disappear during the movement? Does the I finally disappear with suddenness, or is there a certain sequence?

Such questions have to be kept in mind. So far as our experiments with pictures of animals are concerned, our data (pp. 127-138) include *only those responses* which demonstrate the variety and the types of responses. The *donkey and the manger* (see fig. 6) were placed before the background in such a way that the distance between the left foot of the manger and the forefoot of the donkey was 20 cm. The manger has a yellowish green color, the donkey's color is a darker green. The

Stern, W.   *Psychologie der frühen Kindheit.*   Leipzig: Quelle & Meyer, 1914.   Pp. XII+372.

Kerschensteiner, G. M. A.   *Die Entwicklung der zeichnerischen Begabung.*   München, C. Gerber, 1905. Pp. 508.

See also: Downey, J. E.   *On the reading and writing of mirrorscript.*   Psychol. Rev. 1914, *21*, 408.

left ear, the nose and the belly are light yellowish. The S were allowed to look at these pictures with constant or roving fixation the way they wanted. (The same holds for the other pictures.) The exposure time was in most cases 15 sec.

The deer (fig. 3, the end of the hindfeet, the lower part of the body and the mouth are whitish; the tail, the horns, the contour and several spots are black, the rest is orange,) and the *wild boar* (darker green than the donkey, the back and the head are blackish green, fig. 2) were hanging during the exposure, the upper part of the body being ca. 15 cm. from the upper edge of the background. The other pictures were standing. The *tiger* (fig. 7) had the same orange color as the deer except the black stripes and some whitish places on the belly, on the front part of the body and on the hind-legs. Some remarks concerning the color of the other pictures follow: kangaroo (fig. 10): perfectly white with black contour and spots, buffalo (fig. 8): somewhat more darkish than the wild boar, duck (fig. 9, not cut out): bright green head and neck, brownish breast, bluish and brownish tints on the wings, porcupine (fig. 1, not cut out): brownish with black quills, dog (fig. 5): white and black, hyaena (fig. 4, not cut out): white and black spots. The data include a great many of the records concerning the donkey (27 subjects) and the deer (27 subjects). From the records concerning the other animals only those are included which will throw light upon certain problems or on certain individuals. (See pp. 135-137.) There are some records which illustrate the behavior of the I if not one,

but a whole set of animals has been exposed at the same
time.

Donkey and manger (fig. 6)

Lil 15 sec.—11 min. (could see it indefinitely.) S sees a
greenish donkey with the ears straight up; the right
ear somewhat lighter; black nostril and black eyes;
tail hanging straight down; a black outline around
the whole and the bottom of the body somewhat
lighter.

S sees (glance wandering from the donkey to the
manger) the green manger, the black outline, the
"strange feet". ("But the feet do not look like
that. There is nothing like that.") "That may be.
But that is the way I see it." ("Can you bring
manger and donkey together?" S is somewhat surprised.) "Perhaps I can." S now sees two don-
kies, the one standing before the manger with one
front leg lifted, the other at the old place. (E
shows the picture.) "The upper part of the manger looked like that." (E removes the picture.)
"I see the picture again." (Now E takes a colored
picture as a background.) S draws the contour of
the donkey on the background. ("Can you describe the parts of the picture where the donkey
is?") "When I see the donkey I do not see the
picture. When I see the picture, I do not see the
donkey." ("But some objects of the picture are
only partly covered? Can you tell?") "I can't.
I just see the donkey." (E introduces a pencil
from the left.) "No, I do not see the pencil. I
see only the donkey.—But it *must* be possible."
After a while S remarks) "Now I see the pencil
lying *on* the animal."

Seh a. 15 sec. S sees 1. the greenish manger, 2. the
greenish nose; nothing else.

b. 15 sec. S sees—"I looked purposely at the donkey, I see him better"—2 ears; nose, the upper

outer edge of the body; a dark outline around a greenish yellowish color; the mouth and the right ear somewhat lighter; S does not see the forefeet. S sees the manger somewhat lighter; a dark outline around it.

c. 15 sec. (donkey and manger together; the manger placed under the donkey's nose.) S sees the whole form of the donkey's head, the ears; the forelegs; a part of the manger; the whole appears greenish.

d. 5 sec. (ab lib.) S sees "most of the body now;" a dark outline around the *whole* body. "¾ of an inch from the back down I lose the color."

Rin 15 sec.—Can see it as long as she wants to. (During the exposure S looks first from the donkey to the manger and then back,) S sees the whole donkey and the whole manger; the upper part of the manger much lighter; does not see much detail. ("Can you bring manger and donkey together?") S sees the manger and the forepart of the body together; does not see the forelegs; the forepart and the manger now have a somewhat higher position on the background. S finally sees only the head and the upper part of the manger; then the head loses the eye. (E shows the donkey.) "My head was much bigger."

Zeh 15 sec.—8 min. The manger and the donkey appear to S to be the same distance; the ears straight up; "the hind legs aren't together; the forelegs are apart—I remember that it was not so"—; the eye and the nostrils appear to be dark spots; the tail somewhat indistinct; the whole is light yellow in color. S does not see the dark contour. ("Can you bring manger and donkey together?") "The donkey is moving. I do not know whether that is in my imagination or not. But now I really *see* it. It is indistinct. They have come together. The ears are not so straight. The head is hanging down a little." (The S looks through a transparent red paper.) "It loses its proportions." (Now the whole is dark brownish.)

Laj a. 15 sec. (The background is white.) S sees nothing.

    b. 23 sec. (ad lib.) (The background is gray.) S sees an outline of the donkey and the manger. (Eye-movements.) ("The donkey is hungry!") "The donkey becomes colored. The ears move." S believes that the movements appear without her intention, "without thinking."

Dem a. 15 sec.—Can see it as long as she wants to. S sees the manger and the donkey in the original color; the dark spots; the outline; the same position. "I have to think and to feel with the animal. I identify myself with him. It is as if I had two noses. A big nose grows out of my nose. (S indicates this by a movement of her hand.) I even feel into a square. It has life. I have to think to get it. It develops from one point."

    b. —(8 days later.) (No exposure. "Can you get the donkey and the manger again?") S gets the outline of the donkey at once; it becomes more definite at every moment. "Now I see the eye, now the nostril. The ears are just as distinct as before. Now it is colored; now I get the manger." (S sees the same detail as 8 days before.)

Wel 15 sec. S sees the donkey "a light color"; does not see the ears and the eye; cannot see the manger. ("The donkey is hungry.") "I see that his head is bent. But there is no manger." (E moves the background from 50 to 100 cm.) "It is getting bigger." (E raised the window shade at this point.) "It disappears." (The shade in the former position.) "I see it again."

Jus. 15 sec. The outline of the donkey and the manger

appear greenish in color; the ears straight up; the
eye whitish; no tail. ("Can you bring manger and
donkey together?") S sees them together; "but
the ears are not straight now."

Kas 15 sec.—6 min.   The donkey and the manger appear
to be greenish in color. "The manger is not so
plain. The donkey is more distinct." S sees the
ears, the outline of the nose (not the eye and the
nostril.) ("Do you see the dark outline around the
animal?") "Yes, I do." ("Did you see it before
my question?") "Yes, I did. I am quite sure."

Sel a. 15. sec.—1^{15}min. (S looks several times at E
during the exposure.) The manger and donkey
appear equally distinct to S: greenish color; sees
the ears and forelegs; "the hind legs not together," "a dark outline around the whole," no
eye and no nostril; the manger.

b. 15 sec. (S looks at the donkey, then at the manger, then at the donkey again.) S sees the same
as before but the hind part of the body is darker
than the middle part.

c. (During the exposure the donkey performs certain movements. "Can you bring the donkey to
the manger?") S sees the donkey moving to the
manger. The animal is eating there with ears
laid down. S only sees the forepart of the body
with the forelegs. It is perfectly quiet. (E removes the donkey.) S sees the donkey standing
there and the manger that has not been removed.

Nit a. 15 sec. S sees "both as they were," the two
objects appear light colored; the complete contours; does not see the spots for the eye and the
nostril. Then loses the manger. Finally sees
only the foreparts of the donkey, the head, the
ears, the forelegs; but not the rest.

Col a. 15 sec. S sees a bluish outline of donkey and
manger; disappearing and reappearing, no detail.

b. 15 sec.—(manger and donkey together; the manger placed under the donkey's nose.) S sees the I periodically. First period: "Half of the head is in the manger. He is bending his ears over like that. (S indicates the position of the ears.) The whole has a greenish yellow color. Perhaps there is some blue in it." Second period: S sees manger and donkey apart. "They are perfectly blue."

Gil a. 15 sec.—4¹⁰ min. S sees an outline of the donkey and the manger in the original position; the forelegs apart; the hind legs together; "the manger quite distinct;" "there is no color, it is like a black shadow." S does not notice the contour of the animal. (The I disappears; after its reappearance the S sees the donkey to the right and the manger to the left.)

b. 45 sec. (ad lib.) S sees the donkey in the original position but purple in color; "the ears tipped a little;" the hind legs together as though one leg; the forefeet walking; a grayish white contour. S does not see the manger. S sees the manger appear and the donkey disappear. Then the manger vanishes and reappears.

Sut 15 sec. S does not see the manger clearly, sees the donkey "kind of dark;" "two feet" (meaning that the fore-feet are together and the hind-feet together). The I then suddenly turns upside down (180°) and has a higher position on the background. S then brings it "back into the right position.

Low a. 15 sec. S sees the outline of the donkey, "but I do not see the legs." "I see the manger quite distinctly." The whole is blue. S does not see the eye and the nostril.

b. 25 sec. (ad lib.) "There is a blue color around the ears and the legs. It ought not to be that way, but it is so. Some parts are darker." (S looks away, then looks again at the I). "The blue is still there."

Suh a. 15 sec. The donkey and the manger appear to be a light gray color, somewhat lighter than the original color; no detail, but the general outline.

b. 60 sec. (ad lib.)—15 min. "I could see it all day." S first sees the green manger,—"How does that happen? I paid special attention to the donkey!"—sees the dark contour; sees the donkey "without color" and without the contour. ("Imagine the donkey is hungry.") "The *head* of the donkey becomes green. (S shows signs of surprise.) Now the head is moving. The ears fall back. He seems to be eating. Now the donkey has a black contour." (S is intensely observing, then): "The black contour fades away." ("How about the green?") "It is much more vivid than the original color."

Mar a. 15 sec. S sees nothing, then: "I do not know whether I really see something or whether it is in my imagination." (S "tries" a while.) "No, I really do not see it."

b. 20 sec. (ad lib.)—10 min. "Could see it as long as I want to." S sees the manger; sees the donkey— "exactly as it was"—it appears to be a "yellowish green color; the manger not very plain; the donkey without the black contour; a dark spot—"that must be the eye; there were several dark spots, but I do not see them"—the two front legs together; the two hind legs together; the tail hanging down. ("Can you bring manger and donkey together?") "He is really eating! His head comes down to the manger. The whole thing moves in this direction." (S is very much surprised). "Now I have lost him." (S looks around; eye movements). "Now the donkey is where he was at first. He is standing still." S believes the movement was caused by my question. "I made no conscious effort to bring them together. The minute you finished your sentence the donkey flashed to the manger. I think my mind did that unconsciously."

Wen a. 15 sec.—20 sec. "I see a vague outline of the donkey. The 'greenish' belly is more distinct."

b. 30 sec. (ad lib.)—20 sec. S closes his eyes and sees the donkey "much more clearly than before. He is moving."

c. 15 sec. (10 days later.) "I see just a yellowish shade; no definite shape at all."

(Deer fig. 3)

Wen a. 15 sec.—10 sec. So sees a yellowish orange shade; "no clear shape."

b. 12 sec. (ad lib.) S sees the head, the fore- and hind-legs; no tail. The general form is not distinct. The color is a yellowish orange.

Suh a. 15 sec. S sees a very indefinite shape that appears to be a "faint yellow color. It seems to be moving."

b. 1^{15} min. (ad lib.) Se sees a blue outline alternately appearing and disappearing.

c. 4 sec. S sees a yellow I "running three, four times across the background." Finally it becomes smaller.

Gil 15 sec.—40 sec. S sees consecutively an outline of the deer in the following colors: yellowish-orange, purple, black, purple. Then the deer is finally "purple all over without any variation."

Kas 15 sec.—6 min. S sees the deer in the original color; "the fore-feet apart"; "the hind-legs quite distinct"; "the head very bright and clear"; sees the ears and the horns; the whole hind-legs yellowish. (After 4 min.:) S sees only the outline. (1 m. distance.) "The deer has not become any bigger. It stays the same size."

Wel a. 15 sec. "I see a vague, blurred shadow. It isn't the original color." The shadow seems to be darker than the background.

    b. 45 sec. (ad lib.)—60 sec. S sees a dark blue outline; sees the hind—and forelegs, the horns and the ears ;"seems to move."

    c. 60 sec. (ad lib.) "I get nothing."

Dem 15 sec. S sees the dear in the original color; does "not get much detail"; sees only the white parts of the hind legs. "It moves a little."

Maq a. 2 sec. "I see the head and the ears. They are dark. It is gone."

    b. 2 sec. "I see the head. It is yellow. And I see the hind-legs. They are darkish-white. I don't get the rest."

    c. 2 sec. "I see the middle part of the body and the neck. The neck is yellow. I don't see the head but can see the tail."

    d. 10 sec. "I get nothing."

    e. 10 sec.—40 sec. "I see the head and the front-legs. Now I have the hind-legs. The head is yellow. The rest is more indefinite."

Nak 15 sec. S sees a "quite blue" outline. The shape is very indistinct. "I saw the deer at 3 different places."

Zeh 15 sec.—3^{15} min. The deer appears to S a "kind of yellowish color." S sees the fore—and hind-legs; the head "with something on it"; the tail. "It's all the same color." S does not see the dark contour.

Mar a. 15 sec. "Could see it as long as I wanted to." (5 sec. after the beginning of the exposure S looks at E as if he were bored.) "That's long enough." S sees the deer in the original color; "the belly has the same yellow color"; "the two hind legs are together;" "the hind part is a little darker"; "the forelegs are not together"; sees the tail, "but it is darker than the rest of the body;" "the ears and the horns are somewhat darker;" "I can't see the eye, just the yellow head."

    (1 m. distance) "It is no larger, but much

plainer and brighter." (1^{50} m. distance) "It's
the same size." ("Imagine it is running.") "It
is a running position. It is really moving." (50
cm again. E places a red transparent paper on
the I). "I can't see through the paper. I can
see the deer on it." ("Fixate this pencil and
notice what happens.") S first sees that the pencil covers the deer "just in the middle"; then S
suddenly sees 2 deer, one on the right of the pencil, one to the left. (The deer are on the background.) ("Close your left eye.") "The left
deer disappeared. The right one is still there."
(S is surprised.)

b. 2 sec. (The picture of the deer is placed about
half way between the observer and the background: "in the air.") "I can see him in the air.
But what is that? I can see trees and woods. I
didn't think of it. It came all of a sudden. And
the deer has hair." S sees the same with one *eye*.

Tiger (fig. 7)

Mar 15 sec. S sees the black stripes in the yellow; the
bent tail; the "stomach and belly somewhat lighter"; indicates the position of the "right hind-leg";
sees the eye "a different color on the mouth"; the
black contour; measures the distance between front
and hind-legs. (After comparison with the picture): "I don't understand why it should be smaller."

Ret 15 sec. S sees a "light blue outline"; but not the
white of the stomach. "I don't see the gap between tail and hind-legs."
No detail.

Wen 15 sec. "I just see a general shape. The whole
thing is yellow. The legs are like one mass. I
don't see any black stripes."

Wild Boar (fig. 2)

Nak a. 15 sec. "I can't see anything. But I can imagine how he looks."

b. 15 sec. "Now I see nothing but a roundish white circle."

Laj 15 sec. S sees the boar the same color—"perhaps a little darker"—; does not see the black contour. "But now he seems to be at the left." (Turned 180°).

Porcupine (fig. 1)

Wen 30 sec. S sees—"after trying hard"—a bluish animal without any details.

Duck (fig. 9)

Low a. 30 sec. S sees the whole outline; the wing; the legs; the greenish color at the neck; the eye.

b. 20 sec. (ad lib.) "It is the same. But now I have a little color on the wings—it is bluish-red. It is green at the neck. The legs are yellow." (After 1½ min.) "Now I see just an outline."

Wen a. 30 sec.—15 sec. S sees "a pretty vague outline"; has the green of the neck; does not notice other colors.

b. 30 sec.—10 sec. S sees the same outline again; the green of the head, the blue of the body. "The whole is not very distinct."

Hyaena (fig. 4)

Seh a. Hyaena without head. 15 sec. S sees "the bottom parts and the legs, but not the rest." ("Try to get the head." S tries): "I can't do that."

b. 60 sec. (ad lib.) "I see the whole thing; but the line is not so good. The hind legs are very clear. I see the spots between the legs. I don't get the spots near the top line. I have a very indistinct outline of the skull."

c. Head of the hyaena without body. 15 sec. S sees the head clearly; can supplement the rest of the body; measures the distance between fore— and hind-legs correctly.

Kangaroo (fig. 10)

Maq 15 sec. S sees the kangaroo in dark; no detail.

"Now the whole outline has gotten small." S finally sees only the hind legs and the tail.

Buffalo (fig. 8)

Maq a. 15 sec. S sees the forepart of the body, in reddish color. "It is like a horse." The I disappears. After its reappearance the head of the animal is bent down.

b. 20 sec. (ad lib.) S sees the "whole animal." The I fades gradually away. Finally S sees only the head.

A group of animals

Rin a. 30 sec. (On a gray paper lying before the S 6 pictures arranged as follows:

1. donkey	2. wild boar
3. deer	4. tiger
5. kangaroo	6. buffalo

S sees I of 1, 2 and 6 in a greenish color, 3 and 4 in yellowish-orange, 5 whitish. "The kangaroo is most distinct. And then the deer and the tiger." ("Change places of the deer and tiger." S does it; eye-movements; S remarks during this process): "Now the deer overlaps the tiger.— There! it's done." (Paper 90° to the right; the I go with the ground. Then 180°). "I still see the kangaroo, the deer, and the tiger. I have lost the deer. The tiger is still there. It is somewhat hazy." S loses the tiger too and sees only the kangaroo. ("Turn the kangaroo upside down.") S sees the kangaroo in the original position in the upper right corner of the ground. (E puts up the ground in 50 cm. distance. After 7³⁰ min): "I still see the tail and the hindlegs very plainly. But I've lost the ears. The kangaroo seems to be smaller than the original one. All the animals seemed to be smaller." (E shows the picture beside the background for 5 sec. S compares): "No, it seems to have the same size. Now, it's getting bigger. I did not cause that consciously." Horizontal distance hind legs—end of tail (9.5 cm.) : 8.8 cm. Horizontal distance hind legs—(6 cm.) : 6.4 cm. (After 1 min. the same distances) hind-legs—tail (9.5) 8.4 cm., hind-legs (6 cm.) 6.6 cm.

b. (5 days later) (No exposure. A gray ground as before. "Would you get the kangaroo again?") S—looking intensely at the ground—reports about an intermediate state between imagination and visualization. "Now I have visualized that. But the lower part is more prominent; it seems out of proportion. The hind-legs and the tail are perhaps too big." S sees a definite white—lighter than the gray background; no black contour.

Distance hind-legs—end of the tail
　　　　　(9.5 cm.)　: 10.5 cm.
　　Hind legs　(6 cm.)　　: 　6.8 cm.

Jus 30 sec. (On a gray ground before the S
　　　　　1. donkey　　　　2. wild boar
　　　　　3. deer　　　　　4. tiger
　　　　　5. kangaroo　　　6. buffalo)
S sees 1, 2 and 6 in greenish, 3 and 4 in orange, 5 black. S is able to change places of 5 pairs correctly.

Suh 30 sec. (Before the gray background 1. wild boar, 2. buffalo.) S sees only the head of the buffalo and the hind parts of the boar. From this "center" the S develops the forepart of the boar and the hind parts of the buffalo, but does not see the head of the boar very plainly; sees finally the two animals completely.

III. *EXPERIMENTS WITH SILHOUETTES*

The pictures used most frequently are fig. 22 and 24. These two pictures, fig. 22 (10 x 11.5 cm.) as well as fig. 24 (16 x 20 cm.) are silhouettes. Unless otherwise noted

Fig. 22

Fig. 23

Fig. 24

the exposure-time for fig. 22 was 30 sec., for fig. 24 60 sec. and the distance of the background 50 cm. Fig. 23 shows only the part of a silhouette that was 18 by 29 cm. The records included are especially those for pictures 22 and 24. The group of observers consisted of 17 S in both cases. See pp. 140-152.

The special problems involved in eidetic experiments with pictures are stated above. Some points, however, must be noticed to appreciate fully the statements contained in the records.

1.   The *same* pictures are used for children and adults. (One must take into consideration the results concerning the apprehension of pictures obtained e.g. by Meumann, Stern, Schröbler, J. Schrenk.[1])

2.   Certain results of the Aussage-psychology have to be recalled. Stern[2] e.g. found that $\frac{2}{5}$ of the items rightly recalled were *spontaneous* reports of the S, $\frac{3}{5}$ had to be obtained by questions.[3]   An investigation of eidetic phenomena, however, with reference to fidelity of report would fail to recognize the character of the problems in the eidetic field.

III.   *EXPERIMENTS WITH SILHOUETTES*
Picture 22

Gil a. 20 sec.—40 sec. (During the exposure a yellow outline appears around the main objects of the picture: boy, tree, alligator.) S sees the alligator with mouth, legs and tail; boy with legs and

---

[1]Schrenk, J., *Über das Verständnis für bildliche Darstellung bei Schulkindern,* 1914.

[2]Stern. W., *Die Aussage als geistige Leistung und Verhörsprodukt. Beiträge zur Psychologie der Aussage* I. Leipzig: Barth. 1903-04. Pp. 541.

[3]Compare. Jaensch, E. R. 33, p. 85.

arms; arms are "not complete". "The whole is purplish gray."

b. 40 sec. (ad lib.)—10 sec. S sees the boy and the snake, coiled around the branch; the tree; does not see the landscape in the background. The whole is purple, but the eye of the alligator is white. (I disappears, then reappears.) S sees the same; it appears to be grayish white. Then: the snake disappears, next the boy, finally the alligator.

Ret a. 30 sec. "Just the outline of the cut, nothing else."

b. 45 sec. (ad lib.)—60 sec. S sees the outline of the cut; the alligator, the tree; the branch with boy and snake; does not see the forelegs of the alligator. Color: a kind of light black. Looking at one part of the picture, the other parts disappear.

Wel a. 30 sec. S sees nothing.

b. 1 min. 20 sec. (ad lib.)—10 sec. S sees a whitish alligator and tree; does not see the cut, but sees the two outlines on the gray background.

Maq 30 sec.—2 min. 30 sec. S sees white alligator and child; the tree to the right; does not see the trees in the background.

Laj 30 sec. S sees two distant white trees; a "black mountain" between them; the alligator, boy, snake, and tree are black. "Everything is moving except trees and mountains. Now the trees seem to move in the wind." The alligator has sometimes two legs, sometimes four. The big tree has two branches where the branch with the boy is. (E shows the original picture: "Tell me the difference!") "The mountains are not black; the palms aren't the same distance. The two little branches were above the boy."

Low a. 30 sec.—30 sec. "I see the cut; the whole picture is dark; I see the outline of the alligator and the tree; I don't see the boy. Now I can't see anything. The smaller branches of the tree had a real dark color. The trunk had only a dark outline; it had a kind of round appearance."

b. 1 min. 45 sec. (ad lib.) S sees only "the big trunk itself"; a brown color around the tree; then sees the snake with four coils (one small coil), but does not see the branch around which the snake is coiled.

c. 30 sec. S sees the alligator (with mouth and teeth), the snake, and the boy. The figures having a white color are in a purple cut. The palms in the background are not visible. S gives the order of appearance:

    1. Purple cut which is bigger than the original one;

    2. White alligator;

    3. White snake ⎫

    4. White boy   ⎬ in the air

Lin 30 sec. S sees the tree at the right; two small branches; the big branch with boy and snake; the head of the boy very distinctly (indicates the position of the boy's legs and arms correctly); the alligator with two forelegs, with mouth and teeth; the grass and the water; the trees in the background. All of the figures are black. S does not see the I so clearly on a white background; much more distinctly on a gray background. S looking through transparent red paper: "The whole thing is darker, but I can see all the details."

Rin 30 sec. S sees the tree, the child, and the alligator; indicates the position of the boy's legs correctly; sees the mouth of the alligator and one foreleg; tries to see the snake but does not succeed; sees several branches on the tree for a short time; does not see the palms in the background; does not see that the boy is touching the branch; does not see the boy's eyes and mouth. ("Can you make the alligator move?") "Yes, he is moving; his legs are moving. Now the boy is moving too." S looking at E: "I can see the picture on your face."

Suh 30 sec. The boy and the tree appear to be dark. "The boy is struggling and moving all the time. I don't see the rest." ("Try to get the alligator.") After 1^{30} min. concentration S sees the alligator; first the head with the open mouth and the tail, then the rest of the body. S does not "get" the trees in the background. The big branch is just long enough for the boy to hang on it. S therefore does not see the rest of the tree with the snake. ("How did you get the alligator?") "The boy was most distinct. I even saw his feet with the toes. Then I tried to get the mouth of the alligator. A fold in the background (S shows a very indistinct fold) helped me to build up the whole animal. I always start from one point. In this picture the trunk at the right is such a point." ("How about squares?") "I always get the whole square at once. I don't start from one side."

Seh 30 sec.—3 min. "The first thing I have is the outline of the card. The second is the tail of the alligator, the third the child. I have to build up the rest. Now I see a black line to the right. (Does not remember that there was a tree.) At the left in the background there is a dark spot (apparently the snake's place). The boy is most distinct."

Dem a. 30 sec. S sees the head of the alligator; "a little of the black mass of the boy"; the whole is covered with colors. (During the exposition the picture was also covered with colors); therefore nothing is clear.

b. 50 sec. (ad lib.) S sees "nothing except white lines between the mouth of the crocodile and the boy." (S calls that the "central point of interest.")

Ton a. 30 sec.—30 sec. S sees "bright spots where alligator and the boy are."

b. 50 sec (ad lib.) (During the exposure S makes eye-movements). S sees "a more distinct shape of the alligator, the snake, and the boy"; does not see the trees in the background nor the big branch; the objects are whitish. (E moves a pencil from the left into the I.) The I disappears. S believes the movement to be the cause of the disappearance. (E removes the pencil and places it in front of the background.) S now sees the image; can tell what part of the image is covered by the pencil (e.g. the tail). (E places red transparent paper on the I on the background.) S does not see the I: "It is covered up." (S holds the paper before his eyes.) "The white seems to be purple; the dark stays dark. It is very hard to look at the picture that way."

Lil 30 sec. S sees the alligator with "a curly tail"; "that kid" with mouth and eyes; the snake; "the big tree at the right"; "a couple of palm trees" in the background. All figures are dark. ("What is most distinct?") "The little boy and the alligator are most distinct." (S shows the position of the boy's arms and legs correctly; counts eighteen teeth in the lower jaw of the alligator (correct!), draws the upper jaw; sees the white spot on the upper jaw.) ("Where are the feet?") "I don't see the feet at all; they are in the water. I see two forelegs and one hind leg." (S draws the part of the body with the hind leg correctly.) S sees the grass; the water; the snake with three coils; two trees in the background having one trunk. (E shows the original picture. It is lying before the S. "Tell the difference.") "I didn't see the two or three trunks in the background, nor did I see the white eyes and the tongue of the snake. I didn't see the bush in

the foreground and the two branches of the tree."
S (looking at the background) sees the I again;
notices some changes in favor of the real picture:
tongue and eyes of the snake, white lines on the
hind legs of the alligator; cannot get the branches.

Picture 24

Kas 60 sec.—9 min. S sees one dog to the right; the
door to the right; the man pushing the car; the
woman with the umbrella; the church; the trees in
the background to the left, the lamp post to the
left; the square behind the lamp post. The objects
are dark and appear one after the other. S sees
the woman most distinctly; but does not see any
detail; cannot get the other objects, e.g. the other
two dogs.

Jus 1 min.—10 min. 20 sec. S sees a black church, a
black wagon before the church; the man with the
car; several objects: two combs, one pair of scissors in white; the lady with the umbrella (white
with black tilt); "the little man with the hat"
(white and blackish); one big man with black collar; two boys playing; the man at the corner looking at them; the two trees before the church.
("How about the color?") "The trees are white."
S sees the lantern pole to the left (white), the
house to the right (white); the dog to the left
(white). "I don't see the other dogs." ("Can you
bring the dog to the little man?") "Yes, I can.
The dog is biting him. The man is crying, he is
lifting up one leg." ("Can you bring the dog to
the woman?") "No, I can't." "It's all gone now."
(E shows the picture. "Tell me the difference.")
"I didn't see the dog in the middle and at the right,
the two houses in the background, the boy with his
hand in his pocket and the lantern pole to the
right."

Wel a. 60 sec. S sees nothing.
    b. 45 sec. (ad lib.)—1 min. 15 sec. S sees a whit-

ish oblong with darker figures; sees the woman and the two men at her right; does not see the umbrella; sees also the two men to the left; no detail.

Dem 60 sec.—7 min., but S could see it much longer. (During the exposure S sees different colors on the picture; they prevent—as S believes—a clear I). S sees the man with the car; the woman with the umbrella; "the man with the silk hat," "the little fellow's head and shoulders." The woman is most distinct. At first there is a movement of the arm and the umbrella, but then nothing moves. The figures are dark.

Maq 60 sec. S sees the woman with the umbrella; the man with the stiff hat, the poster to the right having the form of a square, the church. The church was black at once and stayed black; the rest first white then dark.

Laj 60 sec. S sees three dogs; the man and the car; the woman and the umbrella; the little man touching the arm of the woman; "the tall man with the stiff hat"; the house at the left with three trees; the car at the corner and the man standing there looking at a couple of boys; two combs ("some teeth are broken"); a pair of scissors; the lantern pole to the left. ("What do you see in the background to the left?") "There is a house with three chimneys; a row of trees before it. Before the church I see a car with a horse." ("How about the wheels of the car?") "I see two wheels, but I can see through them." ("Look at the wall of the house to the right.") "I see a poster; but I can't read the letters." The objects of the I are dark.

Zeh 60 sec.—8 min. S sees dark figures on a light cut; a man pushing the car; "a man with head bent," "a woman with something, probably an umbrella"; a lantern pole to the left (S draws the upper part correctly); "a sort of building in the background" (place of the church). S does not see the small man touching the woman, but remembers him; does not see the children and the other persons; the dogs; the house. S reports the things he remembers. ("What do you see most distinctly?") "The car with the man and the other man are most distinct." ("Did you get all objects at once?") "No, I didn't. Even such a simple figure as the deer doesn't appear at once. I have to look quite a while to build up the whole thing. Here I saw (1) the car, (2) the man pushing the car, (3) the man whose head is bent over, (4) the woman. The rest is vague, but it *is* there."

Seh 60 sec. S gives the order in which the objects appear: (1) the piece of paper, (2) the woman, (3) the house to the right, (4) the steeple, (5) the buildings to the left. "I don't see the car. There are a couple of dots. The dogs and the other persons are dots too." S sees only the steeple, but not the rest of the church; sees the dark parts of the lantern pole to the right, but not the lamp itself.

Sel 60 sec.——5 min. (During the exposure S remarks that she would be unable "to see this picture again. There is too much detail.") S sees—"I can see more than I thought I was going to"— (the objects of the picture appear dark:) the three dogs; the woman and the umbrella; the small man touching the woman; the boy pushing the car; the young man with his hands in his pockets; the church; the row of trees at the left; the two buildings at the left; the house at the right; the two lamp posts; the grip. (E shows the picture.) "The dog at the left was in the middle."

Lil 60 sec.—30 min. could see it longer if necessary. S (begins describing at once) sees the woman with the umbrella; the boy pushing the car; "the little man with the derby hat"; the man to the right; the two boys playing; the man with the shovel looking

at them; the church "with a big steeple"; the row
of trees to the left of the church; the two houses
at the left; the house to the right with 'Entr'; the
lantern before this house; the second lantern to the
left. ("Can you draw the long big globe of this
lamp?") "There is no long big globe around this
lamp. That is at the right." S sees three dogs;
the dog to the left with his mouth open. ("Do
you see the white collar of the dog in the middle?")
"No, I don't. This dog is perfectly black." ("How
does the woman look?") S sees the necklace (indicates the position of the necklace correctly); the
white eye; "the funny hat with white spots"; "the
pretty tight belt." ("Do you see the car?") "There
is no car at all." S sees the white hand and the
derby hat of the small man clearly; does not see the
gloves and the hat of the man to the right; sees the
cigar before him. ("What is falling down?") S
sees two combs one of which has lost several teeth;
a pair of scissors (S indicates the correct position
correctly). ("You see the man pushing the car?")
"His head is down, his hands are like that (S indicates the position of the hands incorrectly). ("And
the car?") S sees some boxes; recognizes a nine
on one box. "There are some marks on the other
box; they are letters." S does not see the wheels
very clearly; sees the whole of one wheel; sees parts
of the other wheel. (A drawing of the car shows
boards around the car.) ("You see the two
boys.") S indicates the position of the arms and
legs of these boys correctly; then indicates the
position of the man at the corner "who is using the
shovel as a cane"; shows the position of the pole
of the car correctly; does not see the two spades
on the car. "I can't see the big trees in front of
the church. I wonder why I don't see the en-
trance." ("Look at the dog in the middle of the
picture. How many legs do you see?") "I see

three legs." ("What is the position of the head?")
S shows the position of the head correctly. ("How
about the tail?") "The tail is between the two
hind legs, it is a little shorter than the legs." ("How
about the tail of the dog at the left?") S draws
the form of this tail correctly; sees one hind-leg
and two fore-legs. ("How about the collars of
these dogs?") "The dog at the right has a collar
and so has the dog at the left." S draws the two
lanterns correctly; but omits the knob on the lantern at the right. (E shows the picture. "Tell
the difference.") "The church was much bigger.
There seemed to be certain displacements in the
background. The lamp post at the right stood on
the sidewalk. I didn't see the big trees in front
of the church nor the little car. I couldn't see
"Richmond" and the other letters on the poster.
The man at the right had a cigar, no gloves and
hat. I didn't see the two spades on the car at the
corner. The little dog at the right was bigger.
The umbrella had no hook. The figures all looked
dark just as they do here."

Lil (after three months, no exposure). S sees the "woman with the umbrella in her right hand. She is
standing like that." (S indicates the position correctly). "There is a fellow running with his car,
his right foot in the air. There are some things
on his car. The man at the right has lost his cigar;
it has fallen nearly to the ground. There is a little
man standing beside the woman. I do not see the
white of his eye. To the right is a theatre. Above
the door I see 'Entr'. At the left of the door there
is a poster. Before the door there is a lantern
pole. The globe appears to be in the form of a
hexagon. I see the scissors very plainly. They
point down to the ground. In the background there
is a church. A row of trees can be seen to the left
and in front of the church. There are three boys,

playing marbles or something like that. (S indicates the position correctly). There is a man looking at the boys. He has a pipe in his mouth. Behind him is one of the little street-cleaning cars.
A shovel is sticking in it. The car is standing at the
corner of the street. The corner runs like that.
(Indicates direction). At the left are some buildings. I do not see any details. In the foreground
I see three dogs. A little dog is standing in the
middle and is watching the scene. They all look
at the scene. I recognize some of the labels on the
car. A nine is standing out. I forgot the fellow
at the left. He has his hands in his pockets and is
looking toward the car. He has a kind of checked
vest."
(E remarks: "Look at the woman!") "She looks
like an old-fashioned woman. The skirt is running
straight down. She has a kind of plume on her
head. I see the pearl at her neck." ("Look at
the man to the right!") "His stiff hat is falling
down. The hat is entirely black." ("Draw this
hat.") The drawing shows that S sees the opening of the hat in the same way as it is in the original picture. "His arms are both in this position."
(S indicates that both arms are lifted.) "I do not
see his eyes but I see his white collar." ("How
about his right hand?") "I see nothing there."
("How about gloves?") "I do not see them"
"The little fellow between this man and the woman
looks unconcerned. He is a little fat man. Well,
I see more than the scissors. There is a comb.
Its teeth are pointed down." ("How about the
car?") "I can see four spokes plainly." (S draws
them.) "The boy who is pushing the car has a
messenger cap on. His hands are like that." (S
indicates the position correctly.) "His right foot is
put backwards." ("Why does the car stop?")
"He is running against the sidewalk. The side-

walk runs like that. (S indicates the direction
correctly.) ("Notice the corner!") "I see nothing there." ("Do you see a rock anywhere?")
"Yes, I do now. I did not see it before your question." ("Look at the dogs!") "They are black,
only the right one and the left one have white collars. The dog on the left has a curled tail.
His mouth is open. I see his four feet. It's a
terrier. The tail of the dog in the middle is hanging straight down. The dog on the right is the
biggest one." ("How about the boys?") "There
are three. One is kneeling down. The boy on the
right has his right arm in the air." ("How about
the street-cleaning car?") "I see one wheel. The
handle is pointing in this direction." (Correct).
"One shovel is sticking in it." ("How about the
lamp-posts?") S indicates the form of the globes
correctly. He thinks that the globe at the right
has the form of a hexagon. ("How about the
theatre?") "I see 'Entr' plainly; the door, but
do not recognize the lettering on the poster. It's
oblong. No, it isn't." (After a certain pause:)
"I think that the left lower corner is torn off. I
am not sure." ("How about the church?") The
drawing of S indicates that certain parts of the
church can be seen to the left of the steeple. (E
shows the picture. "Tell the difference!")
"The little fellow was facing me. The hat was
farther down. (The stiff hat of the man on the
right.) The position of his arms was different.
The church was nearer, the trees seemed to be
smaller. There are only two boys. The man had
no pipe. The size of the dogs is different. The
boy on the left was running harder. There are
eight spokes, but I saw some spokes of the other
wheel too. I did not see the handle of the door."

IV. *EXPERIMENTS WITH DIFFERENT KINDS
OF STIMULUS MATERIAL WITH REFER-
ENCE TO CERTAIN PROBLEMS OF PER-
CEPTUAL PSYCHOLOGY.*

In the following experiments we started from
Jaensch's statement that the laws for eidetic phenomena
are the same as in normal perception. If we have here
only "quantitatively different" laws it must be possible;
(1) to test the "reality" of visual AB, (2) to investigate
certain problems of perceptual psychology. So far as the
last point is concerned one will see that the phenomenology of AB is of secondary importance. The central
fact is the *problem* with its implications.

A. *Exner's experiment.*

Exner[1] says: "Ein weisses Feld wird durch 1-2 mm
dicke Linien in Quadrate von 1 cm. Seitenlänge einge-
teilt. In ein solches weisses Quadrat klebte ich eine ebene
Kreischeibe aus farbigem Papier, deren Radius nähe-
rungsweise dem eines in das Quadrat eingeschriebenen
Kreises gleich ist." Now Exner did not see a colored
circle but a colored square. One may doubt whether
diffusion of color (Exner) will explain this phenomenon;
perhaps it is to be traced back to a certain "Angleichung",
assimilation of forms which is conditioned by the struc-
turation of the form in question. M. Wertheimer's difference between "guten, prägnanten Gestalten" and
"schlechten Gestalten" has to be kept in mind. In Exner's
example the square-form is "zwingend", i.e. compelling,
has "assimilating power" This assimilation may be

---

[1]Exner, S. *Studien auf dem Grenzgebiete des
lokalisierten Sehens..* Arch. f. d ges. Physiol., 1898, *73,*
117.

more easily observed if the paper-form is replaced by a colored "shadow-form." (Compare Köhler's[2] contention that "a certain weakness of the conditioning stimuli" favors the "Tendenz zur Prägnanz der Gestalt".)

According to Jaensch—and the report of many of our observers seem to indicate the same thing—the colors of the AB have the loose structure which Katz[3] ascribes to "Flächenfarben". In our experiments the AB of a circle (fig. 14) was projected on a background with the contour of a square (fig. 13). The diameters of the circles used were 1.5; 2; 3 and 4 cm., the contours of the corresponding squares 2, 3, 4 and 5 mm. Yellow and black colors were used. The number of the S were 10. The records (pp. 153-155) report on only *one* series with the 4 cm.—circle, since no difference could be found in the other series and in the experiments with 1.5; 2 and 3 cm.-circles.

The question was: is the square filled up? If so at what size does the assimilation take place?

A. *Exner's experiment*

Sel 10 sec. (black). S sees the black circle which fits into the square.

Rin a. 10 sec, (black). S sees a white circle; she has to fit it into the square. In near and remote distances it becomes bigger.

   b. 5 sec. (yellow). S sees a yellow circle which is somewhat lighter than the contour. "The circle has a kind of substantial color."

---

[2]Köhler, W. *Die physischen Gestalten in Ruhe und im stationären Zustand.* *Braunschweig*: Vieweg & Sohn, 1920, Pp. XX+263.

[3]Katz, D. *Die Erscheinungsweisen der Farben.* Zsch. f. Psychol. 1911. Ergänzungsband VII.

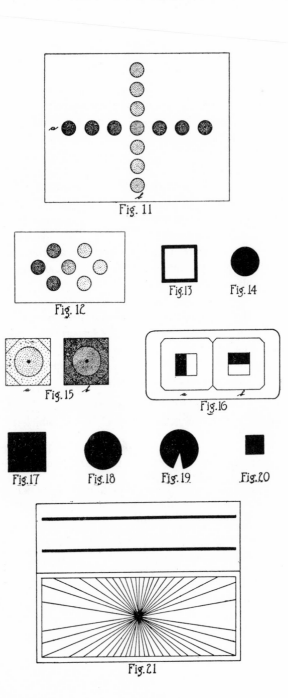

Fig. 11

Fig. 12

Fig.13

Fig. 14

Fig. 15

Fig.16

Fig.17

Fig.18

Fig.19

Fig.20

Fig.21

c. 10 sec. (black square instead of circle.)   S sees a "light square"; fits it into the contour; turns dark.   (E turns the ground 45 degrees to the right):   The AB remains in the same relative position.

Maq a. 10 sec. (yellow)   S sees a "light yellow" circle, "but it does not quite fit.   It's too big."

b. 10 sec. (yellow).   "The same."

Wel a. 10 sec. (black).   S sees a white circle: "the circle is smaller."

b. 10 sec. (black).   S first sees a black circle; this circle turns white and becomes smaller.

c. 10 sec. (yellow)—10 min. 30 sec.   S sees yellow circle (smaller); becomes lighter and bigger.

Gil 10 sec. (yellow)—40 sec.   S sees the yellow circle; this circle fits into the square.   Then the left and lower edges of the square turn white, the rest stays yellow.

Nak a. 10 sec. (yellow).   S sees a purple circle; it fits into the square.

b. 10 sec. (black).   S sees a white circle; it fits into the square.

Dem a. 10 sec. (black)—1 min. 15 sec.   The black circle fits into the the square; becomes suddenly bigger.   The S fits it into the square again. "The color looks like scintillating sparkles."

b. 10 sec. (black).   S sees the black circle; it fits into the black square.   There are, moreover, two black circles and two white squares.

Col 10 sec. (black).   S sees an intermittently appearing white circle; it becomes bigger when more distant.

Kas 10 sec. (black). S sees a white circle; it fits into the square.   It becomes bigger in near and remote distances.

B. *Fuchs' cross-figure*

Wilhelm Fuchs[4] investigated systematically the influence of *Gestalten* upon colors. In his experiments a cross figure similar to our figure (fig. 11) was used. In our figure circles of 2cm. diameter are pasted on a piece of white cardboard. (In the records: V.P. = vertical position, H.P. = horizontal position. See p. 157). In V.P. the circles of the vertical row are greenish-yellow and those of the horizontal row yellow, the central circle being of a shade between greenish-yellow and yellow. If the greenish-yellow row is "aufgefasst" as *one* row the center circle becomes greenish-yellow; it becomes yellow if the yellow row is "aufgefasst" as being *one* row. (The same phenomena can be observed if the two rows have complementary colors and the center circle is gray.) Even the color of the AI of such a cross is determined by the preceding "Auffassung", and a change of the "Auffassung" in viewing the AI changes the color of the center circle.

Starting from Fuchs we tried to investigate these phenomena with AB. The question was: in what way does the "Auffassung" *during* the exposure influence the colors in the AB? Some preliminary tests showed that we could hardly get a group of observers trained well enough for these Auffassung-experiments. The following course was followed: no Auffasung was prescribed, the S had to look at the cross for 10 sec. without fixating it. (Distance: 50 cm.) We used 20 S. The data

---

[4]Fuchs, W., *Experimentelle Untersuchungen über die Aenderung von Farben unter dem Einfluss von Gestalten. ("Angleichungserscheinungen.")* Zsch. f. Psychol., 1923, *92*, 249.

included on pp. 157-162 illustrate characteristic phenomena observed.

B. *Fuchs' cross-figures*

Gil a. V.P. 10 sec. S sees "two yellow lines" then separate purple circles.

     b. V.P. 10 sec. Separate yellow circles (6 sec.); then purple circles. "The purple ones stays in the same place."

Nak a. V.P. 10 sec. S sees the "dark oblong", but no circles.

     b. V.P. 30 sec. (ad lib.) S sees "purple circles" and "purple stripes" alternately.

Dem a. V.P. 10 sec.—Could see it indefinitely. Horizontal row always yellow, sometimes "just a stripe"; vertical stripe first blue, then also yellow. "Something of the white background, but not the oblong."

     b. H.P. 10 sec. S sees the outline of the white cardboard, but no circles. "I gave attention especially to the white background."

     c. H.P. 15 sec. (ad lib.) S sees all the yellow circles; "they move with the eyes;" the background is whitish; this whitish color has the form of a diamond. Then the vertical and the horizontal row appear alternately. Then the yellow circles turn dark. "And they stay dark unless I think about them." S gets yellow circles.

     d. V.P. 5 sec. S sees yellow cross, but no definite circles.

     e. V.P. 10 sec. S sees a yellow cross again, but no circles; then blue circles appear.

     f. V.P. 1 min. 45 sec. (ad lib.) (S "tries" with a certain effort; eyes almost closed.) S only sees the white card, but no circles. "I looked at the whole card."

     g. V.P. 60 sec. (ad lib.) (S gives special attention to the circles.) S does not see the circles; tries several times; then suddenly the circles appear

on a gray ground *lying on the table.* The circles
have the same shades as the original ones.
("Imagine that the center circle fits into the
verticle row.") Now the center circle turns the
same shade as the circles of the vertical row.
("Can you fit it into the horizontal row?") The
center circle becomes the color of the horizontal
row. S is unable to place the circles on the
background standing in front of her. Then the
circles flow into two yellow oblongs. Then oblongs and distinct circles are alternating. Afterwards only yellow oblongs can be seen. ("Con-
centrate upon the center circle!") The center
circle appears:

(Drawing of the S.)

"It is a deeper yellow, and is bigger." Finally:
"Now the little ones appear—they are brighter
and smaller."

(Drawing of the S.)

Kas V.P. 10 sec. S sees a greenish vertical row with
one definite circle. This center circle becomes
gradually smaller and lighter. (Measurement:
1.5 cm. in diameter.)

Maq a. V.P. 10 sec.—1 min. 50 sec. S sees the card with
two rows of distinct "blue" circles; the center
circle is more distinct and bigger; then blue turns
into yellow; the card disappears; the horizontal
row is more distinct; finally

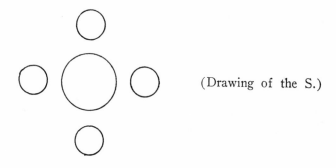

(Drawing of the S.)

b. H.P. 25 sec. (ad lib.)—1 min. 45 sec. S sees the V.P.; blue circles which turn into yellow. "The middle circle is not colored, but there is a yellow halo around it."

Laj   H.P. 10 sec. S sees yellow light circles; the form of the card board. "All the circles have the same color."

Wen a. V.P. 10 sec.—25 sec. S sees "a sort of pale yellow cross"; no different shades of yellow; the circles could be distinguished; the background seemed "somewhat lighter."

b. H. P. 20 sec. (ad lib.)—10 sec. S sees "a yellow blur" having the form of two rows; the white background has the form of a diamond.

c. H.P. 10 sec.—20 sec. S sees a yellow cross; the circles are not definite. The circles turn blue.

d. V.P. 10. sec.—20 sec. S sees "a yellow cross, it does not turn blue." The background again takes the form of a diamond.

Ret a. H.P. 10 sec. S sees a light purple cross; no circles. "The horizontal line is more vivid."

b. V.P. 20 sec.—1 min. 30 sec. S sees "a light purple cross"; the vertical line is "more solid". S concentrates upon the center circle:

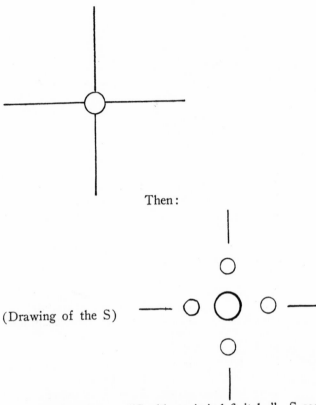

Then:

(Drawing of the S)

Suh a. V.P. 10 sec.—"Could see it indefinitely." S sees
light blue circles, then two rows alternating:
"the horizontal stripe is dimmer and wider." At
2 m distance: S sees the two rows simultaneously; the circles of the vertical row; "but they
are still bigger than the original ones."
(Measurement: 2 cm. in diameter.) (E turns
the background to the right). The "yellow cross
in light color" goes with the background.

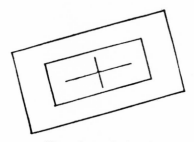

(Drawing of the S)

(E causes the background to fall down.) The cross disappears. (S tries to see it again.) S sees a yellow cross. "The one top-circle stands out." S "builds up" the whole form from the top; indicates the degree of "clearness":

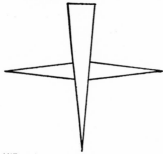

("Look at the center circle.")

Now:

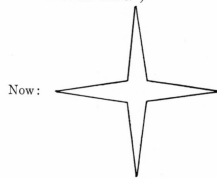

The background.

Rin   V.P. 7 sec. S sees two rows: the horizontal is
        yellowish-green, the vertical somewhat darker
        and clearer. "The vertical row seems to overlap
        the horizontal."
        S does not recognize different circles; S sees the
        white card. ("Please, concentrate upon the cen-
        ter.")   The center circle arises and becomes
        brighter than the vertical *and* horizontal line.

Sut   V.P. 15 sec.—15 sec. S sees a "dark cross on
        whitish paper"; no distinct circles; the back-
        ground seems to have the form of a diamond.

Seh   V.P. 10 sec. S sees "a big blur. It's like a shad-
        ow on the background."

C. *Hering's illusion.*

If only "quantitatively different" laws hold for eidetic
phenomena it must be possible to get "striking" results
by making use of optical "illusions" which are unknown
to the S. Thus the 20 S used stated that they were un-
familiar with Hering's illusion we experimented with.
The cardboard with two black lines (11 x 26 cm)— see

fig. 21—covering the card with the crossing lines was standing before the background. After 15 sec. the front card was removed and the S had to project the two lines on the card with the crossing lines. The data (pp. 163-164) showing the great variety of phenomena also make clear why we did not apply other illusions.

C. *Hering's illusion.*

Nak 15 sec. S sees "two pinkish lines." (Position and curvature as in Hering.)

Gil a. 15 sec. S sees "two straight black lines. Now the background has disappeared. I only see two black lines." Then the background reappears with two yellow lines. These lines are disappearing and reappearing.

 b. 10 sec. S sees "two straight black lines." Then they "turn yellow with a black outline."

Lil 15 sec. S sees "two black lines. The lines are bent toward the center. The lower line is somewhat more bent." S believes that the "black spot," the center, attracts the attention.

Sel 15 sec. S sees two black straight lines "in the same position." (E moves the background to the vertical position.) "The black lines are also vertical."

Seh 15 sec. S sees "two greenish yellow lines. They are straight." (E moves the background to the vertical position): "The lines do not move with the ground."

Sut a. 15 sec. "I cannot place the lines on this background." S tries but does not succeed.

 b. 15 sec. (S sees "four dark lines" during the exposure). S cannot get the two lines. "All the small lines run together somewhere far behind."

Ret 15 sec. S sees "two white bent lines." (Position and curvature as in Hering.)

Wen 15 sec.—10 sec. S sees "two dark straight lines.

The upper line is more noticeable; the lower is barely perceptible."

Laj   15 sec. S sees either "one black line" (bent as in Hering) or the "ends of both lines."

Dem   15 sec. S sees two "black lines. They seem to be straight." Suddenly S sees them in an oblique position.

Rin   4 sec. S sees "two straight lines." (E moves the background to the vertical position). "The lines move with the ground." (E moves the ground to the former position.) "Now I see three backgrounds with black lines, the real one and two others."

Suh   15 sec. S sees "two black lines. They are not bent. I am disturbed by the center."

Wel   15 sec.—2 min. S sees "one white stripe just through the center." The line is straight. (E turns the background slowly to the vertical position). The line jumps back into the horizontal position at 45°.

    b. 15 sec.—4min. S sees two white straight lines which afterwards turn dark. (E turns the background to the vertical position.) The line always jumps back into the horizontal position at ca. 80°.

D. *Ragona Scina's experiment.*

For the description of Scina's procedure I refer to Helmholtz.[1] In our experiments the form *reflected* by a red glass was a black circle. The forms to be observed *through* the glass were two concentric black circles. At the beginning, however, the glass was absent. The S (10 subjects were used) was allowed to look at the white card with the two circles as long as he wanted. Then it was taken away and the S developed his I at the same

---

[5]Helmholtz, H. *Handbuch der physiologischen Optik,* 3rd ed. 1909, Hamburg und Leipzig: L. Voss.

place. After this the red glass was introduced. In all cases the I disappeared. In further experiments the glass was introduced very slowly and certain pauses were made. Thus the I was partly covered by the glass. Now after having introduced the glass fully only three observers saw something. Lil and Mar stated that the circles stayed dark. Dem saw "bluish" circles. No data concerning this experiment are included.

E. *Jaensch's "Kovariantenphänomen."*

In the interpretation of eidetic phenomena the Marburg school lays much stress upon the factor of attention. Investigations with AB concerning the so-called "Hering-Hillebrandsche Horopterabweichung" (49) lead to the conclusion that "antagonistic processes of attention" (Mach) and "Aufmerksamkeitswanderungen" (variations of attention) explain this phenomenon. Reversals of position and the so-called "Kovariantenphänomen" are also explained by this factor.

By means of the following procedure the "Kovariantenphänomen" can be observed. If one exposes three parallel threads a, b and c in such a way that they seem to hang in one plane and displaces *a* slightly, then *c* also seems to be displaced either in the same or in reverse direction. Tables including measurements with five observers[6] illustrate that the displacements when working with AB are greater than when the actual threads are used.

---

[6]Freiling, H., Jaensch, E. R. und Reich, E. *Das Kovariantenphänomen, mit Bezug auf die allgemeinen Struktur—und Entwicklungsfragen der räumlichen Wahrnehmungen.* Zsch. f. Sinnesphysiol., 1923, *55,* 47.

In general, it might be asked: is attention really the deciding factor? One often applies the term attention when it would be better (1) to pay more heed to the phenomenology of the field in question (2) to see whether or not the structure of the object is responsible for the appearance of "attention".

In analyzing Jaensch's method the following points must be noticed:

1. The three threads were 5 cm. apart (16, p. 276), the thickness of the black threads was 0.4 mm. (49, p. 61). At the beginning of the experiment the middle thread was 15 cm. (49, p. 70) behind a screen. All three threads could be seen through a slit 5x20 cm. (49, p. 69). Behind these threads a gray background was placed. The distance is not given.

2. So far as the technique of measurement is concerned (see 49, p. 72 and 16, p. 276) it is not stated whether the "measuring-threads" which have to coincide with the I-threads have always been introduced from behind or not.

3. The fact that sometimes a certain "set of attention spontaneously (ungezwungenerweise) occurs" is observed but not analyzed. (49, p. 350). Moreover, we are not told how it is possible that—having a definite "Auffassung" whose importance is stressed—"Aufmerksamkeitswanderungen" take place.

Our question, therefore, was: are not the objective spatial relations responsible for what according to Jaensch is due to attention and shifts of attention?

We started from Jaensch's setting and changed one factor: the *slit* through which the threads can be seen. In our first series this slit was 2.5 x 20 cm. (screen I similar to Jaensch's) in the second series it had the following form and dimensions.

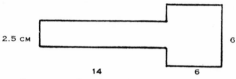

By such means the thread c appeared behind the right opening. The S was instructed to fixate b and to have a comprehensive "Auffassung" of all three threads. The distance between the bridge of the nose (head-rest) and the middle thread was 1 m, the gray background being 40 cm. behind the threads. The three threads a, b, and c, were moved about until in the judgment of theS they seemed to lie in one plane. (Jaensch's "zero-position.") After the exposure they were dropped and the I of a, b, and c could be seen. After this the middle thread (b) was introduced from behind and theS had to state when coincidence between the I-thread and the real thread took place. Then leaving b in place, the same is done with either a or c. Thus the S sees two real threads and one I-thread. E put down the number of mm. the two real threads were behind the "zero-position." (See e.g. AI_1, p. 169). Now the E moved back one of the real threads (see AI_2) and then introduced a third thread in order to determine the position of the I thread. (See AI_3).

In series A and C (see p. 169) slit I was used, in B and D slit 2. Subjects Mar and Lil seemed the only promising S, but they had no more time available. Dem had great difficulties in distinguishing I-thread and real threads. The lateral distance between a, b and c was always changing. Gil always saw the third thread as at the distance of the background. Some of the values for Gil and Zeh are included whereas S who saw the threads always moving are not reported on.

E. Jaensch's "Kovariantenphänomen."

		A—Screen I			B—Screen II			C—Screen I			D—Screen II		
		a	b	c	a	b	c	a	b	c	a	b	c
Lil													
I	1	62	62	IT	60	60	IT	61	61	IT	60	60	IT
	2	162	62	IT	70	60	IT	66	61	IT	65	60	IT
	3	162	62	62	70	60	62	66	61	64	65	60	64
II	1	66	66	IT	63	63	IT	63	63	IT	36	36	IT
	2	66	166	IT	63	73	IT	63	68	IT	36	41	IT
	3	66	166	66	63	73	65	63	68	64	36	41	39
III	1	IT	45	45	IT	61	61	IT	61	61	IT	67	67
	2	IT	45	145	IT	61	71	IT	61	66	IT	72	67
	3	46	45	145	63	61	71	66	61	66	67	72	67
IV	1	65	IT	65	33	IT	33	61	IT	61	75	IT	75
	2	165	IT	65	133	IT	33	66	IT	61	80	IT	75
	3	165	65	66	133	33	33	66	62	61	80	79	75
Gil													
I	1	170	170	IT	80	80	IT						
	2	270	170	IT	180	80	IT						
	3	270	170	Before the background	180	80	Before the background						

II	1	90	90	IT	120	120	IT						
	2	90	190	IT	120	220	IT						
	3	90	190	Before the back-ground	120	220	background Before the						
Zeh													
I	1	80	80	IT	94	94	IT						
	2	180	80	IT	194	94	IT						
	3	180	80	46	194	94	50						
II	1	85	85	IT	88	88	IT						
	2	85	185	IT	88	188	IT						
	3	85	185	42	88	188	45						
Mar													
I	1	65	65	IT	52	52	IT	90	90	IT	79	79	IT
	2	165	65	IT	152	52	IT	95	90	IT	84	79	IT
	3	165	65	65	152	52	53	95	90	94	84	79	79
II	1	67	67	IT	66	66	IT	83	83	IT	57	57	IT
	2	67	167	IT	66	166	IT	83	88	IT	57	62	IT
	3	67	167	67	166	166	66	83	88	83	57	62	58
III	1	IT	64	64	IT	17	17	IT	51	51	IT	72	72
	2	IT	64	164	IT	17	27	IT	51	56	IT	72	77
	3	64	64	164	17	26	27	56	51	56	72	72	77
IV	1	50	IT	50	57	IT	57	43	IT	43	42	IT	42
	2	60	IT	50	67	IT	57	48	IT	43	47	IT	42
	3	60	50	50	67	57	57	48	44	43	47	47	42

V. EXPERIMENTS WITH THREE-DIMENSIONAL FORMS.

A. In a series of preliminary experiments we made use of flowers, vases, and watches. The data (pp. 171-178) contain the observations concerning the I of *candles*. The candles used were red or yellow. Their height was 15 cm., their diameter ca. 2cm. Below the top (with the white wick) were seen ca. 12 ridges running in a spiral downward from right to the left. The ridges at the bottom ran in perpendicular direction. During the exposure the candle was standing on a gray ground before the background used. (Exposure time in most cases 10 sec., see below.) The S was told not to fixate the object but just to look at it. The words applied by the S in describing the I are not changed in the records.

V. *Experiments with three-dimensional forms.*
A.

Sub-ject	Exposure-time Duration	Color of stimulus	Appearances observed
Zeh	10″ 22″	red	red color, ridges; becomes bluish, candle has a "sort of oblique position!"
"	10″ 30″	red	greenish blue, intermittent appearance.
Lil	10″ ad lib.	red	red color, ridges, whitish wick, not intermittent.
Wel	10″ 80″	yellow	yellow, standing there "like a column"; becomes gray and fades away.
"	10″	yellow	yellow, then yellow with dark in the middle, finally the whole is dark and is

			moving to the background; sees it on the wall.
Mar	$\dfrac{10''}{\text{ad lib.}}$	yellow	yellow, does not appear at once; takes quite a while to develop it; sees ridges and wick, indicates the position of the ridges correctly.
Wen	$\dfrac{10''}{12''}$	yellow	indistinct yellow, "no variation of color"; sees ridges, candle does not appear at once.
Suh	$\dfrac{10''}{50''}$	yellow	yellow, three-dimensional, sees wick and ridges
"	$35''$	yellow	yellow, three-dimensional, sees wick and ridges; then a purple shadow on the background.
Ret	$\dfrac{10''}{2'}$	red	red candle, "standing there", no wick, no ridges, not moving, looks at me while talking, cannot see it *through* blue paper, but in front of it.
Ret	$\dfrac{10''}{50''}$	yellow	yellow 5 sec., then purple, standing somewhat above the ground in the air, no wick, etc.
Jus	$\dfrac{10''}{25''}$	yellow	yellow candle with wick and ridges for 4 sec., then bluish, appears on the background.

Col	$\dfrac{10''}{40''}$	red	green intermittenly; "like a picture", no wick, no ridges, moving.
Fow	$\dfrac{10''}{50''}$	yellow	purple color, no wick, no ridges, moving with the eyes.
Low	$\dfrac{10''}{40''}$	red	pink color 15 sec., even the wick is pink; "little sort of cuts" (ridges); then green, on the background smaller, not three-dimensional.
"	$\dfrac{10''}{50''}$	yellow	purple, ridges, wick also purple; then it jumps to the background, "standing out" from the background.
"	$\dfrac{10''}{50''}$	yellow	yellow 4 sec., at once on the background; then dark blue, finally light blue.
Nit	$\dfrac{10''}{90''}$	red	1) red candle with ridges, no wick.

. . . . red

2)   2 thin candles

. . . . green

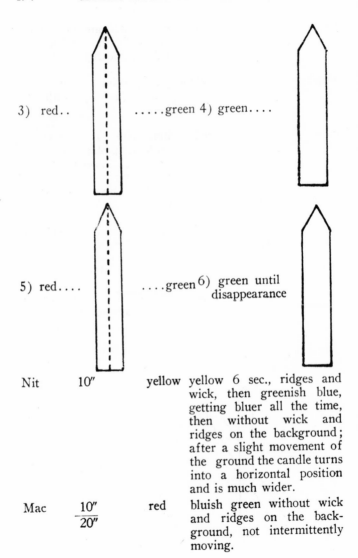

3) red.. .....green 4) green....

5) red.... ....green 6) green until
disappearance

Nit   10″   yellow   yellow 6 sec., ridges and wick, then greenish blue, getting bluer all the time, then without wick and ridges on the background; after a slight movement of the ground the candle turns into a horizontal position and is much wider.

Mac $\frac{10″}{20″}$ red   bluish green without wick and ridges on the background, not intermittently moving.

Ton	10″ / 25″	red	greenish without wick and ridges, moving on the background.
"	4″ / 8″	yellow	yellow 4 sec., turns blue; is standing at the same place, "not smooth."
"	10″ / 18″	yellow	bluish candle, no wick and ridges, persistently.
Bec	10″ / 30″	red	greenish, at the same place; no details, persistently.
Ber	10″ / 30″	red	"three thin candles" standing there, no ridges, no wick,

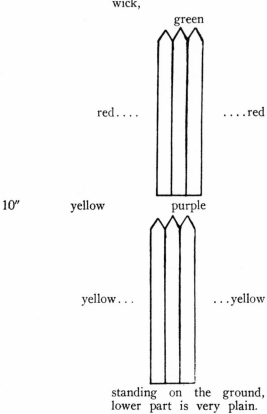

standing on the ground, lower part is very plain.

Dem	$\dfrac{10''}{\text{ad lib.}}$	red	very light red, not moving with the eyes, whitish wick and ridges; right half of the candle somewhat brighter; standing at the same place.
Rin	$\dfrac{10''}{\text{ad lib.}}$	red	red at once, green halo, ridges, no wick; gets green. At a distance of 1.25 m. wider (4 cm.) and shorter, at a distance of 25 cm. 2.5 cm. wide.
Rin	$\dfrac{5''}{\text{ad lib.}}$	yellow	purple with yellow halo which finally disappears, no ridges and wick, at near and remote distances wider; standing before the background, candle is pushed forward with the background, can be moved; at a distance of 3m. 3.2 cm. wide.
Seh	$\dfrac{10''}{70''}$	red	red at once; ridges and wick; the left side somewhat darker (the light comes from the left) be- **comes finally gray.**
"	$\dfrac{10''}{70''}$	red	the same in green.
"	$\dfrac{10''}{60''}$	yellow	left half of the candle, dark, right half yellow, yellow finally disappears; no ridges and no wick.
Kas	$\dfrac{10''}{50''}$	red	greenish, no ridges and no wick; standing in the air.

	$\dfrac{10''}{60''}$	yellow	bluish-greenish, no details; cannot be moved.
Lin	$\dfrac{10''}{\text{ad lib.}}$	red	red at once, "but not so bright"; seems somewhat shorter; ridges and wick; very distinct; cannot count the ridges; no shadow at the right side, becomes brighter before a white background; is pushed forward by the background; the ground goes somewhat into the candle; candle is not round at the point where a ruler is introduced; a red shadow is lying on this ruler; fixation of a pencil held between eyes and candle, the latter changes its form.
"	$\dfrac{50''}{\text{ad lib.}}$	yellow	yellow at once; sees the same details as before; picture as a background; "I cannot see the details of the picture where the candle is. It is not clear." E: "Remove the candle." S is surprised but finally succeeds.
Laj	$\dfrac{10''}{70''}$	red	red, white wick, ridges, indicates the direction of the ridges correctly.
Sel	$\dfrac{10''}{28''}$	red	red at once standing at the same place; wick and ridges; the left side lighter; becomes dimmer.

Sel	$\dfrac{5''}{74''}$	yellow	yellow at once, the same details, can be projected on the background, gets somewhat flat.
Sut	$\dfrac{10''}{2'30''}$	red	red 10 sec., but only the upper part of the candle can be seen, no wick, becomes finally green.
Sut	$\dfrac{10''}{60''}$	red	red 7 sec., ridges, no wick, but the whole candle is seen, becomes green finally.
Maq	$\dfrac{10''}{2'10''}$	red	dark green and red alternating; pink sometimes has a green halo, green a pink halo; when pink, the wick is whitish; when green, it is green; pink has no ridges, but the green has.
	$\dfrac{10''}{1'45''}$	yellow	yellow and blue alternating in intervals of ca 2 sec., sometimes 2 candles at the same time; candle at the left blue, candle at the right yellow. The same details as before.
Gil	$\dfrac{10''}{40''}$	yellow	yellow, then purple, finally dark; no wick and ridges.
Nak	$\dfrac{10''}{30''}$	red	candle red and green; the top sometimes red, sometimes green.
	$\dfrac{10''}{60''}$	yellow	blue disappearing and reappearing consecutively; no details; standing there.

B. W. Köhler's intelligence-examination of anthropoids caused a discussion concerning the "Einsicht" of chimpanzees.[7] Jaensch doubts that the intelligence of a chimpanzee is a function of the "optical field-structure." According to Köhler, having "Einsicht" implies the 'grasping" of the structure of the situation, "das Erfassen eines sachlichen, inneren Bezugs zweier Dinge." Jaensch's experiment intended to prove that in most of the actions of chimpanzees we have nothing but a "dislocation with regard to a goal" is not convincing. (38, p. 195).

What will happen if the arrangement of stick and desired goal object is not:

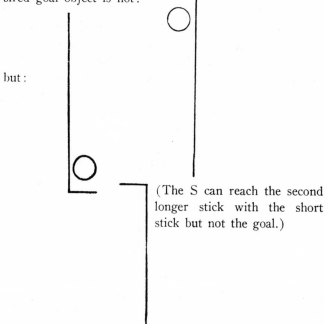

but:

(The S can reach the second longer stick with the short stick but not the goal.)

[7]Köhler, W., *Intelligenzprüfungen an Anthropoiden I*. Abh. d. Preuss. Akad. d. Wissenschaften 1917. Physikalisch-mathematische Klasse.

In trying to reach a goal, what matters is not the *fact* that two objects come together but *what* two objects. And this depends upon the fact that whether the "Funktionswert" of the one object—to adapt Köhler's term—is recognized or not. And that is —Einsicht. Indeed, Jaensch's remark that some of his S got the solution "after brief reflection" about the possibility of the solution is interesting.

Being convinced that the dislocation in the AB will hardly explain the chimpanzee's actions, we have brought out this point. We were, however, unable to carry out the experiment suggested. The short crook (muddy yellow color) was 60 cm. long (diameter 0.6 cm.), the long one 80 cm; the goal was a stopwatch. The S never succeeded in seeing the 3 objects at once in the AB. (Perhaps the spatial relations played a role.)

We therefore decided to use only two objects and to investigate a different problem. On a gray background (30 x 70 cm.) lying before the S. the crook (60 cm.) and the watch were placed in the following position:

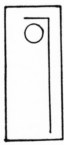

Now the question was: what happens in AB if the ground is moved? Some S saw at least the crook long enough to secure some data. (See pp. 181-183).

B.

Ret 40 sec. (ad lib.) S sees first a shadow of the watch
and then a light blue crutch. Both are entirely
"flat".

Wel 60 sec. (ad lib. S sees a "dark spot" as a watch
(disappears soon) and the stick. The stick is
"blue or dark or blue and dark." "The whole
is flat."

Sometimes S sees an "intense blue" on the
gray paper. And this blue "flows" into the dark

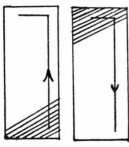

stick. Sometimes the blue color
appears at the other end and the
reverse process takes place.
Width of the dark stick about
2 cm. Width of the blue stick
about 0.8 cm. Sometimes the
left side of the stick is dark, the
right side blue. (E turns the
ground 90° to the right.) "The
stick becomes indistinct. Now I
don't know where it is." (The
ground in the old position:
"Imagine the stick is lying on the ground." Then
E turns the ground 90° to the right. During the
movement S sees an "indefinite something";
"but I can't describe it." Horizontal position.)
"I am sure that I see the long stick, but I am
not sure whether the upper part is there."
Sometimes the right and left part of the ground
are covered with blue. In the original position
the stick never disappeared, in the horizontal
position it intermittently appears. ("What do
you see now?" No answer—a long period of
observation—a process of "recreating.") (The
ground standing in a vertical position before the
S: 50 cm. distance) "The whole sticks to the
place."

Rin 30 sec. (ad lib.) S sees "a light watch and a bluish
crook. Both are a certain height." Watch (oval
form) and crook are connected. (S is surprised).
The watch has no details. (E turns the ground
90° to the right.) "The watch and crook do not
move with the ground. I see them on the table."
(E turns the ground into the former position.
"Now imagine that watch and crook are lying on
the ground." E turns the ground slowly 90° to
the right.) "Now it's going around. I believe
that my thinking makes it seem to move." (E
turns quickly again 90°). "It moves with the
ground." (The original position of the ground,
crook and watch lying on it. "Now look at it and
notice what happens." E turns the ground 90° to
the right.) "It does not move with the ground."

Gil a. 30 sec. (ad lib.)—10 sec. "I did not see the stick.
I only saw a whitish watch. But the knob of
the watch was to the left." The watch seems to
be three-dimensional; it has no detail.

b. 30 sec. S sees "the whole watch and stick."
The stick is purple and the watch is whitish.
The stick is flat; but the watch seems to be three-
dimensional.

c. 40 sec. (ad lib.) "Whitish watch," "purple
stick."

Dem 30 sec. S sees "the stick and the watch in the
original position, color and form;" the dial, the
black rim, the stem (also black); no handles. Now
and then the stick turns purple. (E turns the
ground 90°.) "I lost the watch, and the stick
jumped several times into its original position.
Now it is lying in the horizontal position." (Slow
movement to 180°.) "The stick turns with the
ground." (Quick movement to 270°,) "The stick
jumps into the original position. I'll bring it back."
(S "brings it back," does not know in what position the crook "should be.") (Slow movement to

360°) S sees it in the original position. Suddenly the stick jumps into this position. (S is surprised and "brings it back.") ("Could you get the watch again?") S sees the watch, but it becomes very indistinct the moment she will "take" the watch with the stick. Concentrating upon the stick the watch becomes dim.

4. *INTERPRETATION OF DATA.*

Before discussing the specific data of this study certain general observations should be noted.

1. *In general,* it seems that the Eidetiker dealt with in this investigation do not constitute a material which is apt to furnish reliable data that will convincingly *explain* normal, non-eidetic phenomena and by such means *solve* certain problems of perceptual psychology (e. g. the problem of apparent size, etc.). The interpretation of the data, however, shows that the eidetic phenomena are not entirely chaotic, but are governed by certain "laws" which have, of course, a bearing on many non-eidetic investigations.

2. Since Jaensch's methodological presupposition on p. 80 does not hold for our material it follows that we, starting from *problems* as above stated, did not try to secure data concerning *these* problems. It was always possible, however, to collect observations concerning the phenomenology of the appearances in question. (See p. 88).

3. There seems to be no reason to treat the data of children differently. The phenomena observed are of the same type. (See p. 91).

4. The *single* phenomenon observed does not decide whether somebody belongs to the eidetic type or not.

It might happen that the characteristics of a phenomenon are merely characteristics of pure AI.

5.   Concerning the measurements which played an important role throughout the investigation certain points have to be taken into consideration. *We first hesitated to include the results of these measurments at all:* in most cases it was obvious that the size of squares and of other "meaningless" material was influenced by inner factors, by "will" and by "thinking." Moreover, the fact *that* E does measure a square as well as the *method* of measurement seems to be important although it must be assumed that the method—whether from the outside or inside, whether horizontal or vertical—has *relatively* very little influence in changing the size. One is very often surprised at the exactness with which even children determine the distance measured. The feet of the compass have to be changed 1 mm. or 0.5 mm. In this respect our observations confirm those of Jaensch. (33, p. 20). But there is no reason to take into account the influence of "measurements from the outside" and of "measurements from the inside" (Koffka) if the S explicitly states: "A minute ago it was much, much bigger. Then I narrowed my eyes and made it smaller." (Low at a distance of 150 cm. His AB were not measured, of course). A vertical measurement from the outside, therefore, seemed sufficient.

In spite of this the results of some series of measurements are included:

(a)   Notwithstanding the influence of a great many unknown factors it is hoped that the comparison between individuals may bring out certain points.

(b) Such instances as the case of Ernst M. (49, p. 317) with his extreme lability of all phenomena are not found.

(c) The I always had a certain perceptual givenness. The phenomenon in question *is there* and in many cases the S looks with an expectant, curious attitude: "What will happen?" Thus the S does not influence the I *intentionally*.

Keeping in mind these general points we turn to the discussion of the various experiments.

I A1: *Size at distances different from the distance of exposure.* (P. 101).

In six cases neither AB (10 sec.) nor AI (40 sec.) could be measured, and it should be noted that *four* of them are children. Sometimes the I lasted for only a short time, sometimes they were moving and fluctuating. Changes of size were reported. In three further cases (Fow, Bec, and Ber) no values could be obtained after an exposure of 10 sec. Ber did not get an I at all. The I of Fow and Bec were *not* persistent enough to be measured.

The data I A_1 and the observations made indicate:

1. Pure "Einheitsfälle" (Krellenberg[1]) are not found, since in all cases the AI had the complementary color. (The exposure time never exceeded 40 sec.)

2. In general, the AI do not follow Emmert's law. Only 8 S have the values to be expected according to this

[1]Krellenberg, P. *Über die Herausdifferenzierung der Wahrnehmungs-und Vorstellungswelt aus der originären eidetischen Einheit.* Zsch. f. Psychol., 1925, *88*, 56.

law, and four out of these cases are "weak" cases. (Sut, Ton, Ber, and Bec.)   The incongruity found, however, is of such a kind that the values at the remote distance (150 cm.) tend to be greater.

(The law referred to is formulated by Emmert[2] in the following way: "Die lineare Grösse eines Nachbildes ist . . . gleich der linearen Grösse des Objekts, multipliziert mit der Entfernung, aus welcher das Nachbild betrachtet wird, d. h. multipliziert mit dem Vielfachen der Entfernung, aus welcher das Objekt betrachtet wurde, das Ganze dividiert durch die einfache Entfernung." This

---

[2]Emmert's formulation is to be found in "Klinische Monatsbl. f. Augenheilkunde 1881, *19*. As to the discussion centered around this law see:

Zehender: *Anleitung zum Studium der Dioptrik.* Erlangen, 1856.

Scharwin, W. and Novizki, A. *Ueber den scheinbaren Grössenwechsel der Nachbilder im Auge.* Zsch. f. Psychol., 1896, *11*, 408.

Mayerhausen, G. *Noch einmal der gefässlose Bezirk der menschlichen Retina.* Arch. f. Ophth. 1883, *29*, 150.

Mochi, A. *Neueste Untersuchungen über die Projektion monokularer Nachbilder durch das nichtbelichtete Auge.* Zsch. f. Sinnesphysiol., 1910, *44*, 81.

James, W. *The principles of psychology.*. 1890, II, p. 51.

Alexander, H. B. *Some observations on visual imagery.* Psychol. Rev., 1904, *11*, 319.

Müller, G. E. op. cit. II, p. 379.

Goldschmidt, R. H. *Grössenschwankungen gestaltfester, urbildverwandter Nachbilder und der Emmertsche Satz.* Arch. f. d. ges. Psychol., 1923, *44*, 51.

means $1^1 = \dfrac{1a^1}{a}$: $1^1 =$ linear distance in the AI, $1 =$ linear distance in the original stimulus, $a^1 =$ distance between eye and AI, $a =$ distance between eye and the original stimulus).

3. The deviation from Emmert's law is much more pronounced in the case of AB. (10 sec.)

4. In general, there seems to be a certain tendency to constancy in the remote distances. (But see Maq, Jus, Col and Ton.)

5. There is a certain tendency to enlargement in the near distance. (25 cm.)

This holds not only with reference to the original size (5 cm.) but also if one takes into consideration the *relation* between the size at the remotest distance (150 cm.) and the near distance (25 cm.). It must be kept in mind that the background was moved from 150 to 25 cm. In ⅔ of the AB measured the value in the near distance is greater. The value 2.5 cm. to be expected if Emmert's law should hold was never obtained. Extraordinarily high values (25.2, 13.2) are found.

6. No characteristic difference between the values for positive and negative AB can be found. (The AB measured under *a* were positive, under *b* negative.) Further, there seems no difference between children and adults.

7. Comparison with P. Busse's value (p. 102) brings out the "irregular," at least entirely different behavior of our AB.

I B. *Size-studied at a distance equal to the distance of exposure.* (P. 104).

It must be remembered that the values are obtained in

the above stated way (p. 98). The measurements and other occasional determinations of size seem to indicate:

1. The size of the AB in the isodiastatic constellation is in most cases not identical with the size of the original stimulus, the AB is either smaller or bigger. (Compare Zeman 100, p. 253.)[3]

2. The preceding measurements in the heterodiastatic constellation seem to influence the size of the AB in the sense that an enlargement takes place. There is, however, no indication that the immediately preceding measurement (at 25 cm.) influences the size in the isodiastatic constellation.

3. A comparison with P. Busse's values (5, p. 42) obtained from _8_ observers shows again that the variation in our case is much greater.

4. E noticed that variations within a certain range (up to 0.5 cm.) were often unremarked by the S. The S claimed that the I had the size of the original square.

I C. _Size-studied at a distance equal to the distance of exposure, the background being a picture._ (Pp. 106-107). Our observations and the data seem to show:

1. In the isodiastatic constellation the AB is smaller than the original stimulus when the background is a picture. (The same was noticed when other heterogeneous backgrounds were used. Compare 21, p. 82.) Comparison with I B indicates that it is possible to speak of a "contracting" influence of the picture-background.

2. Positive and negative AB behave in the same way.

----

[3]A study of the author with non-eidetic persons concerning the size of AI in the isodiastatic constellation brought out the fact that AI in most cases have not the size of the original stimulus.

3. In general the values for the vertical distances are greater. Whether that is due to the method of measurement—the vertical distance was determined first and the horizontal later—is not clear.

4. A certain cohesiveness has to be ascribed to the AB. It does not mix with the background. It often happens, however, that the "competition" between background and AB results in the disappearance of the latter after a short duration.

5. More detailed observations with some S (the records of Suh, Dem and Rin are included) show that the *removal* of the picture has not necessarily any considerable influence. The approximate constancy of size (different backgrounds, different positions) in the case of Suh is quite noticeable.

I D Form—the background tilted 45° to the right. (P. 107).

1. There is a remarkable difference in the phenomena observed. Size and form vary from individual to individual.

2. The deformation which is to be expected with AI (78, p. 87) is not typical here.

3. In the case of certain deformations it seems *as if* a real object were exposed. Similar observations are made by Krellenberg with Willi Ma and Ho. We cannot accept, however, his interpreation. In our cases Laj and Nit—*a* as well as *b* might be determined by experience.

4. In general, the AB seems to stick to the ground. (See, however, Rin.)

1 A₂. Color etc. of AB. (Pp. 102-104)

The chief stimulus material used in our investigation were squares. The data included on pp. 102-104 refer mainly to the qualitative side of the phenomena. *Out of many experiments* with squares we have reported about those observations which illustrate either the behavior of the AB of the S in question or a special phenomenon.

Our observations and the data included show:

1.   An exposure-time of 10 sec. is sufficient to get an AB whose duration may vary from a few seconds to an indefinite time. In most cases, however, 10 sec. are not necessary; in some instances a fraction of a second suffices. Sometimes (especially Dem, Rin) an exposure is superfluous. The S "gets with a certain effort" the color he wants.

2.   There are positive and negative AB. Having a constant exposure—time does not imply, however, that the S has only positive AB or only negative AB. (See e. g. Bec.)

3.   If in the AB *no other* color than the *original* one is seen, the phenomenon does not disappear and reappear consecutively. The original color finally "fades away."

4.   The color of the positive AB does not always exactly coincide with the color of the original stimulus. (e. g. Zeh, Bec.)

5.   If *no other* color than the *complementary* one is seen the AB can appear periodically (e. g. Col, Mac) or is persistent (Rin)..

6.   If two different colors are seen it may happen that either the original or the complementary color appears first: (e. g. Maq, Nit.). These two colors are, however, *not always* the original and complementary color. (e. g. Wel, Jus.)

7.   The two colors appear alternately (Maq) or the first color appears for a relatively short time (Wel 4

sec., Gil 4 sec., Wen 10 sec., Low 60 sec.) and for the rest of the time the other color can be seen. This second color in most cases is permanent (Ton), in some instances it disappears and reappears (Wel).

8. The AB either fades away into a "dark" or "gray" (sometimes "bright") color, or the color in question stays to the end. In some instances a gradual shrinking from the square form to a spot is reported.

9. If two colors are noticed at the same time either a "glow" or a "halo" is *around* (e. g. Wen, Ton) or a "spot" is *in* the square. (e. g. Laj).

One may compare Krellenberg's S Tchä (66) and Dr. Ennen's observations. (34). Jaensch sees here "Binnenkontrastphänomene."[4]

11. In general, it could not be found that the color of the AB is influenced by the distance of the background.

In the case of Col, however, all AB got a "whitish" color at the distance of 25 cm. Wel always sees for about 4 sec. a color equal or at least similar to the original color. After this the complementary color emerges and disappears at 25 cm. Then a "brownish" color is seen quite irrespective of the color of the preceding AB. Phenomena of this kind are probably not due to the distance alone. (Col is not color blind).

1 E. *Mixtures of various geometric figures.* (Pp. 111-117).

First the data of S Rin shall be considered. In evaluating the results of this "color-mixture" one has to take into consideration the whole attitude of the S:

---

[4]Blachowski, S. *Studien über den Binnenkontrast.* Zsch. f. Sinnesphysiol., 1913, *47, 291.*

(1) This attitude was on the one hand quite passive; the S looked at the phenomena perceptually *given* with a certain expectant air and was often surprised that things did not happen the way she expected. The statement of the S were evidently *determined* by the appearances *given.*

(2) On the other hand, the S was able to "move" a square, even to see an AB without immediately preceding exposure *if* she wanted.

The E is convinced that the S not only was uninformed about the mixture of spectral light but also that she did not intentionally influence the phenomena reported on. Nothing is said here, however, about the influence the *Einstellung* has had. Experiments with Rin invariably gave the same results on different days. The experiments with *3* squares were *not* repeated for lack of time.

In general, the protocols of Rin seem to show:

(1) Seeing simultaneously 2 or 3 AB it is possible to change the position of one AB without causing the disappearance and a change in the position of the other one. However, a certain attitude ("set") in which the S "umfasst" or "pays attention to" all the AB present, is a prerequisite. Spatial relations seem to play a role: in the case of 3 AB a "side-by-side position" is necessary.

(2) The fact that the AB mix in a constant way (mixtures of 2 squares *always* as on pp. 111-112) proves the "objectivity" and the reality of the phenomena and their independence from the S if one takes into consideration point (1) and (2).

(3) In view of this constancy of the mixtures the fact that there seem to be "deviations" from the laws of color mixture is immaterial.

Deviations of this kind are only apt to raise certain questions. The *AB*-colors are evidently different from the more "compact" and more "substantial" colors of the original stimuli. Often they have evidently, as stated above, the characteristics of Katz's "Flächenfarben." What conditions determine the mixture of these colors in this experiment?—Having 3 or more AB squares it might be asked: do changes of color take place ("Angleichungen" of colors) if there is a Gestalt *with* certain AB colors?

Specifically the observations seem to show:

(1) If one calls the color which is placed upon the other one *A* and the color on which A is placed B it seems that in most cases the mixture has a stronger A—component.

(2) Having 3 colors, it seems to be possible that the third color has an inducing influence upon the color of the mixture of the two other ones (See p. 116 and also Krellenberg).

(3) So far as the process of mixing and the result of the mixture is concerned there is no difference whether the color to be mixed is the original or the complementary color of the stimulus or whether the exposure was monocular or binocular. An exposure is not necessary at all if the S *knows* how the object looks. (See p. 113) (If in monocular vision the AB is seen with the eye to which the original stimulus was not exposed (p. 112) the color depends upon the exposure-time).

(4) The "mixture-square" is enlarged as a comparison with the size of the AB to be mixed showed (p. 112).

(5)   The possibility of determining the phenomena to a certain extent has certain limitations:

(a)   AB and "objective background-square" (p. 113) having the same or a different color—cannot be mixed.

The S does not know "why." It just seems as if the simultaneity of AB and real square evokes certain antagonistic tendencies. Even the *presence* of a square seems to disturb the mixing (p. 113). (Similar phenomena are reported in the Marburg publications; they are, however, not explained. Probably the phenomenological aspect of AB-color and object-color plays a role).

(b)   Black and white AB cannot be mixed. (p. 112). The S thinks that the "contrast" between the two colors prevents the mixture. In this connection it might be mentioned that the gray square used in these experiments was seen "black" in the AB. In fact, the gray square had exactly the same shade as the background on which it was exposed. (See also Dem. p 117). Probably a certain process of "Strukturierung" causes this "square clearly distinguished from the background."

c)   AB of squares cannot be moved or mixed if the original stimuli were sides of a three-dimensional object. (p. 115). It seems conceivable that the S could not *mix* two identical cubes; E. R. Jaensch's and Reich's two S (49, p. 289) could also not mix three-dimensional objects, but only place them "side by side." Our S, however, could not even move the front sides which were all she saw.

(6)   In the process of mixing eye-movements play a role. They always could be observed in VII, p. 116, see also VI, 3, p. 114 but in the latter case certain psychic factors may be important.

(7) Certain "assimilations of form" also occur *in* the AB. (e. g. VI, 5, p. 114; VI, 15, p. 116).

The cases Dem and Lil (p. 117) represent 2 extremes. It is interesting that even Dem who is able to influence the phenomena to a remarkable extent has to "fight such an obstinacy" of the phenomena as appears in the competition of the two colors.

I F. *Mixtures by means of a stereoscope.* (p. 117). Our observations and the drawings on pp. 118-120 show:

(1) The "competition" between the AB and the "real" object seems more pronounced than in Hering (p. 162). In most cases the AB disappears in spite of the longer exposure-time. One has to take into consideration:

(a) The drawing on the left side of the stereoscopic picture appears with a certain jerk.

(b) The observation through a glass or transparent paper was always considered "unnatural."

(2) The different positions of the AB (Suh and Mar draw the normal position) are probably due to shifts on the right-hand cardboard during the development.

(3) The smallness of Jus' AB is the result of one of the "shrinking processes" elsewhere often observed.

I G. *Oblong card filled with geometric figures.* (Pp. 120-122).

(1) No S obtains a long lasting AB which shows approximately the same completeness as the original stimulus (p. 120). Most AB have the short duration of about 4 sec.

(2) It is worth mentioning that in some cases the central parts are most easily obtained and more likely to appear. (Col and Lil).

(3) Very "irregular" phenomena occur. (Maq, Nak, Low).

In general, certain observations during the whole experimental work suggest that meaningless forms, the simultaneous presentation of a large group of meaningless forms, are more likely to cause appearances of this kind. In this connection see also Hering (p. 62) and the data on pp. 157-162. The data on pp. 121-122 throw light on the behavior of extremely "irregular" I.

II. *Experiments with pictures of animals.*   (Pp. 127-140).

The experiments with pictures are more liable to throw light upon the *process* of eidetic vision than other experiments.

(1) Spontaneous remarks while looking at the AB reveals the fact that all S even the children, *sharply* distinguish between the visualization of an object and their own knowledge about this object, between the AB and MI.

(2) In some cases the AB appears at once. (Usually the visualized object does not have all the details at first: a certain sequence can be noticed.) In some instances there is a stage intermediate between "visualization" and "imagination." This state does not always lead to the visualization of the object. (Mar. p. 132).

(3) Exposures after the first exposure do not necessarily cause a greater distinctness and clearness of the AB. Sometimes the AB does not appear at all after the second exposure. It seems as if a lack of interest prevents the appearance. (See also 66, p. 98). In a few instances consecutive exposures result in a "building up" of the AB: every time the AB becomes more complete. So far as the process of "building up" is concerned the

observation of Dem (donkey and manger were exposed 8 days before) is typical: she sees consecutively a vague outline of the donkey, a more definite outline, the eye, the nostril, the color, the manger, the spots, etc. In most cases those parts of the figure which seem most "prominent" and determine the form and appearance are seen first: e. g. the head, the outline. It never happens e. g. that the tail appears first. It has happened in our series that the tail can be seen while the head cannot be visualized. (Maq. p. 134). But this is explainable since Maq who after the first exposure saw the head and the ears of the deer "tried" to get the *rest* of the body. Thus after the third exposure he succeeded in getting the middle and hind part of the body with the tail, but not the head.

(4) There are great differences as to completeness: we have a continuum from an indefinite "blurred shadow" (Wel p. 133) to a fairly accurate AB. Photographic fidelity is very rare. A selective tendency is operating which is very likely to exclude certain parts of the picture. In the AB of the donkey the spots, the nostril, the eye, even the black contour; in the deer the spots, the horns and the tail; in the tiger the black stripes do not appear so often.

The parts which appear are in most cases of different distinctness. Thus the head is often more distinct than the rest of the body.

The fact that certain parts of the exposed picture are more likely to appear and others not might be traced back to several factors. In general, the "AB—value" of a part of a picture is the greater

(a) The more essential this part is for the structure of the figure and

(b)   The more the S "concentrates" upon this part. There are irregular cases, however, which do not follow this rule.

(5)   AB of animal-pictures have a greater tendency to retain the original color than the AB of squares or of "uninteresting objects."

On the other hand there are not only AB in the original and complementary color, but also in colors deviating from these.   Sometimes the AB is positive and negative. (e. g.—white eye, white contour.)

(6)   AB of animal-pictures do not disappear and re-appear consecutively in the great majority of cases.

(7)   Form and color of the original picture very often suffer small modification in the AB.

For instance, the position of the fore—and hind-legs of the donkey differs; the ears are more tipped; the ani-mal shows no variation of color; the black tail and the black horns of the orange deer are orange, etc.

(8)   Movements of the AB—animals (e. g. the run-ning deer; the donkey goes to the manger) are either caused by the "effort," the "will" of the S or happen quite unexpectedly.

These "unexpected happenings" are released in some cases by an outer event, e. g. by a suggestive remark of the E (Mar. p. 132), in some cases by inner factors not controllable.   In the movements caused by the S eye-movements seem to play a role.   (Movement of the don-key to the manger.   See also p. 194).   In some cases the animal disappears during the movement and reappears at the goal.

See in this connection the getting of color (e. g. Laj,

p. 129 and Suh, p. 132) upon the remark of the E: "The donkey is hungry."

(9) The movements observed have a certain meaningfulness.

The donkey is eating in quite a "natural" position, the deer is runing as is "suggested" by the original picture, etc.

In this connection it might be mentioned that Mar's observation (p. 135) has also a meaningful relation to the original stimulus.

(10) The "hanging" exposure seems to favor movements of the AB as well as reversals of position.

(11) Movements of real objects can be observed; but in our series only a few observations of this kind are reported. (See also 15.)

(12) Certain processes of "Einfühlung" or "Einsfühlung" are often involved in the process of visualizing. (Dem, Laj.)

(13) AB regarded through colored transparent paper either disappear, appear *before* the paper or suffer certain deformation and changes of color. The color observed is in most cases not the same as would be seen in normal vision. The S always found experiments of this sort somewhat unnatural.

(14) The process of "fading away" is in most cases a "reversed building-up" process.

In general it seems as if the form is more "essential" than the color. And certain prominent parts of the form stay longer than others (e. g. the head.)

It is remarkable that the last details to disappear are not the geometrically central parts of the body, but the phenomenologically characteristic parts : e. g. head or nose of the donkey, the hind legs and tail of the kangaroo.

(15) In case two objects are exposed (donkey and manger) the distance (p. 125) sometimes seems to prevent the simultaneous appearance of the two I. (See Rin. p. 116).

During the exposure eye-movements could be observed in all cases. Looking at the *AB* it very often happened that the S was fixating either the donkey or the manger. The object not looked at was in this case more indistinct, but *not always*.

(16) The experiments with a greater number of interesting objects are apt to demonstrate certain points better than the experiments with one object:

(a) It is possible to see quite a number of objects simultaneously. A certain concentration, however, seems to be necessary in order not to "lose" one: the eyes wander from one object to the other.

(b) The fact that after a number of displacements which E has asked S voluntarily to make in the AB even children indicate the correct order seems evidently to prove the reality of these phenomena.

(c) The AB of the different objects do not disappear at the same time. The "fading away" of the last animal is the same as stated above.

In the case of Rin it is interesting that during the fading of the last parts (tail and hind-legs) the tail becomes shorter while the length of the hind-legs still increases for a certain while.

The observation often made that the S thinks the AB has the same size as the original stimulus or is bigger, while measurements show that it is actually much smaller, is perhaps of great importance. (See the discussion about the "apparent size.")

The fact that the AB moves with the ground it is lying on will be discussed later.

III. *Experiments with silhouettes..* (Pp. 140-151).

The experiments with silhouettes bring out the same points as under II. Certain processes, however, can be better observed.

1. It is possible to see a very complicated picture in the AB after a relatively short exposure-time, but there are no photographically accurate records. Having a constant distance, big pictures seem to prevent the getting of complete AB.

2. There appears to be a selective tendency always to neglect the same details: in picture 22 the landscape with the palms in the background, some branches of the tree at the right, the grass, even the feet of the alligator; in picture 24 some of the dogs in the foreground, the spectator at the left, the trees in the background, the details of the houses or the houses themselves at the left in the background, the two boys playing, the poster on the wall to the right, some of the objects falling down from the car.

3. The process of "building-up" a picture as well as the process of "fading away" is more marked than in the experiments with single animals.

In picture 22 the space which includes the right leg of the boy and the mouth seems to be the center of the building-up process. Dem, who sees nothing in her AB but white lines between the mouth of the crocodile and the boy, calls it "the central point of interest." (See p. 143).

In the great majority of cases the succession of the parts in this process mentioned is not the succession of parts which are geometrically continuous, but which are phenomenologically characteristic: e. g. after the head of the alligator the tail of the animal appears, but not the big mass of the body (or very indistinct); the boy appears, but not the branch he is hanging on; the snake can be seen, but the branch it is coiled around is not there.

In picture 24 the man pushing the car or the woman or one of the dogs appear first in most cases.

In general, the geometric continuum does not seem to determine the stages of the "building-up"; e. g. after the woman, the man with the stiff hat might appear, and *then* the man *touching* the woman (or he does not appear at all); later the boy with the car can be seen; the dog before him might appear, but not the boy who is almost *touching* his foot.

Why certain parts are "phenomenologically characteristic" is a problem not to be discussed here. *One of* the factors involved might be mentioned: we *see* the *dynamis* of things, it is perceptually given. Only an incomplete and inadequate description will neglect this *dynamis*. Thus e. g., the umbrella, and the dog have a certain *dynamis*. In the AB the umbrella mostly appears, the cypress, however, which has a similar shape and size is never mentioned by our observers. And it seems that this *dynamis* we all see is more pronounced in the AB. The mouth of the alligator, the legs of the boy are moving, etc.

In cases where the state intermediate between visualization and imagination was of long duration and the S did not cease "trying hard" certain characteristics of the background (e. g. a fold in the paper) sometimes helped build up the AB.

4.   Most AB of silhouettes are positive; there are also negative, and negative and positive ones.

Thus the "prominent group" in the middle was sometimes positive and the background negative and vice versa. The fact that the cut (shape of paper carrying the objects) appears at all or even that the cut appears first is in most cases probably due to a certain "Auffassung" of the picture. The S then places the objects "on" or "in" this cut. Very often the S tries in vain to get objects. Most observers do not see the corners of the cut at all. No S reports spontaneously about the color of the "empty space" between the objects. In other words: in the great majority of cases the processes discussed are going on in the "Bildraum," therefore the cut will not be seen at all.[5]

5.   There are certain AB whose peculiar character seems to be explained by the second determinant of the "AB-value" (p. 198). See e. g. Seh, (p. 147). AB of this kind have a certain "atomistic character."

There still remain certain observations where certain factors not controllable play a decisive role.

6.   So far as the attitude of adults and children in describing pictures is concerned our observations confirm the Marburg observations that part of the S enjoyed describing AB. After the object is taken away they begin to talk without being asked to do so; they look with a certain enterprising air at the E just as if they were describing a real scene. (See p. 91). A minority

---

[5]In this connection compare e. g. Peter R. *Studien über die Struktur des Sehraumes.* Hamburg. 1922.

of S, however, are entirely wrapt up in the process of building up and after this in looking at the picture. They hardly look away and consider every question of the E as disturbing.

IV. *Experiments with different kinds of stimulus materials*

The data are chiefly a contribution to the phenomenology of AB rather than to the problems we have set out to investigate.

A. *Exner's experiment* (pp. 153-155).

In the following the points which are better illustrated by the square—and picture-experiments (appearance and disappearance of AB, their color, their duration, etc.) will not be mentioned.

1. In general, no "filling-up" of the surrounding square-form takes place.

Conditions similar to those stated on page 113 seem to be operative. If in remote and near distances the circle becomes bigger, it naturally fills up the square: the *form* of the circle does not disappear.

2. The fact that the S does not at once project the AB into the square explains the statements concerning the "fitting in" of circles.

3. The fact that the circle has not in all cases the original size is interesting with reference to our statements concerning size in isodiastatic constellations. There seems to be a tendency, however, for the size of the "AB-circle" and the original circle to coincide, a tendency which is probably due to the square-form.

B. *Fuch's cross-figure.* (pp. 157-162).

Our observations with Fuchs' cross-figure seem to indicate:

1. There are differences between the looking at a picture and the looking at a figure. In the case of a picture the S sees persons, actions, etc.; in the case of this cross-figure S sees a *piece of paper with circles* on *it*. In many cases the AB therefore contains the circles *and* the white piece of cardboard. The form of this cardboard is sometimes the original one; sometimes an oblong without corners, sometimes a diamond. If the *whole* oblong is seen the circles are likely not to appear at all. After their appearance the outline of the whole can no longer be seen. If at the beginning all circles are seen only a diamond appears, etc.

Some of the factors involved here are:

(a)   the size of the cardboard,

(b)   the kind of "Auffassung." A "piece of cardboard showing a cross-figure" is different from a "cross-figure on a background."

2. So far as the color is concerned the phenomena differ *considerably*. The most important of these differences are:

(a)   All circles show the *original* color.

(b)   All circles have the *same* shade of yellow.

(c)   The colors are the original ones, but the central circle has the color of one of the rows.

(d)   All circles have the same yellow shade which changes into the complementary color.

(e)   One row is yellow, the rest is complementary.

(f)   The two yellow rows appear alternately (the same shade.)

(g)   Two complementary rows appear alternately (the same shade).

(h)   No definite circles can be distinguished, but two stripes—either original or complementary—can be seen.

(i)   One stripe with the definite central circle can be seen.

The yellow of this circle might be "lighter" or "deeper."

3.   In somes cases a conscious "Auffassung" or "Herausfassung" (e. g. of the central circle) causes changes of color and size.

4.   It is noticed generally that a conscious effort of the S to get certain phenomena in the AB is often without result; but after ceasing to try the phenomena suddenly and unexpectedly appear.

Our plan to prescribe a certain *Auffassung* during the looking at the AB did not succeed since the phenomena were too evanescent and fluctuating.

C.   *Hering's illusion* (pp. 162-164).

The experiments with Hering's figure well illustrate the very different behavior characteristics of AB.   They show that we have here not only "qualitatively different" laws for eidetic phenomena, but phenomena which are of an entirely different character.

1.   The curvature which is characteristic of Hering's illusion forms an exception to the general rule.   Generally the two lines are *straight*.   Only in three cases out of *twenty* the curvature is the same as in Hering.   In two cases the lines are bent towards the center.   In two further cases *one* line, about 1 cm. wide, runs through the center.   In general this seems to show that under certain circumstances the form of the real object does not influence the form of the AB.   Other factors are probably operative here: the S is in such a set of mind that he is "willing" to see two "straight lines," or rather,

two lines as they were.   In some cases the S thinks that
the center "attracts" the lines and sees two lines bent
toward the center (see Lil, p. 163).   Or this "attraction"
is so effective that only *one* line is seen (see Wel. p. 164).
It is therefore possible that in the three cases where the
normal curvature is seen a certain "repulsive power" of
the center is considered to be operative by the S.   There
are no reports backing this view but judging from the
totality of our observations it is more likely that a certain
"set of mind" has determined the normal curvature than
the drawing on the background.   (In this connection
compare Hering's and Ragona Scina's experiment and the
experiments with transparent colored paper.)

2.   In only a few cases did the background seem to
be disturbing.   Sometimes it appears three-dimensional.

3.   The nature of the stimulus material exposed does
not explain the variety of colors in the AB.   There are
not only black and white, but also "pinkish," "yellow"
and "yellowish green lines."   (Comp. 23.)

E.   *Jaensch's "Kovariantenphänomen."* (pp. 169-170)
Our data are not sufficient to warrant any general conclusions, they have, however, a certain value:

1.   Columns A and C (experimental setting similar
to Jaensch's) show that Jaensch's "Kovariantenphänomen" can be observed in the AB.   There are—as Jaensch
noticed—observers with whom the process of co-varying
is "positive" (Lil, Mar, Gil) and observers where this
process is "negative." (Zeh)   (In the latter case the third
thread comes *nearer*.)

2.   A displacement of 10 cm. of the real thread does
not always cause co-variation as in the case of Jaensch's
observers.   (Column A.)   A considerable smaller dis-

placement is necessary with Mar and Lil. (5 mm; see 16, p. 53.)

3. The I-threads are *never* in the same place as the original ones. Their position is behind the position of the original threads (in the case of Gil even 170 mm.). Curiously, Jaensch's observers *always* saw the I-threads as the same place as the original ones.

4. Column D seems to indicate that *a* and *b* and not *a* and *c* tend to co-vary. This is probably due to the *form* of the opening in the screen and not to "Aufmerksamkeitswanderungen." Further data, of course, are needed.

V. *Experiments with three-dimensional forms.*

A. (Pp. 171). The data include those observations which we consider to be "typical" for the individual in question. The observations with three-dimensional objects (candles) show:

1. So far as duration, "building up" and "fading away," the colors, etc. are concerned the observations of the different S are in general the same as those which are discussed under I A₂ (p. 189, experiments with colored squares). In the case of 5 S (Ber, Seh, Lin, Jus and Suh) certain differences are noticed: the candles retain the original color, while the two-dimensional squares are in most cases not positive.

2. Most S see the candle, at least for a certain time, in three dimensions. There were 18 persons out of 27 who noticed the ridges. When the ridges appear in a negative AB the conditions of light and shadow are the same as in the original candle. (66, p. 101). Sometimes the candles appear like columns, the ridges and the wick cannot be seen. It is interesting that the AB after it has

lost its three-dimensional character goes from the ground it was standing on to the background.

3. Some S are able to move the candle, in other cases a displacement is impossible. The candle, however, can be pushed by the background. This background may go "into" the candle. An object (e. g. a pencil or a ruler) which is moved through the AB can destroy the three-dimensional character at that place, but not necessarily. The size of the AB and of the object introduced into it of course play a role.

It appears to Dem, who has the AB of a green vase, that the background can be seen vaguely through the vase, sometimes it appears before it. In certain moments the ground seems to be in the vase. "I think that is the way the fourth dimension could be demonstrated."

B. (pp. 181-183). These experiments reveal the same facts as certain observations occasionally made during our work in the "Exner" and "Hering."

1. Under certain conditions the AB can take part in the movements of the ground.

2. A certain attitude of the S is probably a prerequisite.

a. The E asks S to imagine "that the object is lying on the background" and the S tries to cause the AB to participate in the movement of the ground: the AB moves with the ground.

b. The E moves the ground slowly without giving any instruction: the AB is also moving. In other words: —the S has recognized the *meaning* of the movements the E performs. These "silent" instructions or interpretations of meaning in situations are probably of great importance in eidetic investigations.

c. The S is in a certain passive attitude:— what will happen? The AB does not move with the ground. Possibly there are cases when a movement would take place, but we never observed it.

d. The E moves the ground with a certain jerk, at least very quickly; a movement of the AB is not observed. It is possible that the AB suddenly appears at the goal.

3. The behavior of the AB during the movement differs:

(a) it is lying plainly on the ground,
(b) it represents an "indefinite something,"
(c) it sometimes jumps back into the original position.

4. The S's capacity to "determine" the localization of his AB seems to play a role. There are individuals who seem to have no influence at all upon the movement in question. Others succeed to a certain extent: Wel (p. 164) sees the two lines until a position of 80° rotation in counter-clock direction; on a continued rotation of the ground it always jumps back into its original position. Dem, however, is able to take the AB-stick between two fingers and move it, or to bring an AB-cup near to the mouth, so stable are her visualizations.

. . . .

It would be very strange indeed, if the Eidetiker would notice his eidetic disposition first in the laboratory. Phenomena of the above described character influence, of course, the intellectual and emotional life of the individual to a certain extent, and, as it seems, often to a very prominent extent. That does not imply that the individual always recognizes the importance of his AB. Out of the 27 subjects we used, 9 could not report anything concerning the role the AB had played in their previous life. And it seems worth mentioning that 6 out of these 9 were adults. Lil and Wel, who are in this group, belong to our strong cases.

What follows is chiefly based on statements of the S made during the course of our experiments. Nothing was reported by Kas, Ber, Bec, Ton, Lil, Maq, Wel, Fow and Col. It might be noticed that our data include many statements which throw light upon the relations between the Eidetiker in question and his AB. The spontaneous remarks and explanations of the S will sometimes appear somewhat indefinite, but in this case no better information could be obtained.

Let us turn first to the adults. Here especially it often seemed inadvisable to ask for certain kinds of information.

Zeh. Sometimes sees intentionally or unintentionally objects again. In the latter case he is always surprised about their appearance. The I are in most cases vague; only faces are sometimes quite plain. They have not, however, the same substance as real faces; thus he does not confound them with each other.—Once he was in a forest and saw afterwards some of the trees very vaguely.—One day he had an AB of a very ugly woman he had seen in a circus.—His AB help him in memorizing, "but it does not stay for days." In general all I are more dim than bright.

Mar. The experiments show that his AB are in most cases very distinct and show much detail. But they are also subject to many alterations. He asks: "How do you know whether I visualize or remember?" He reports that he has had the ability to visualize from early childhood onward. His playmates have doubted his gift, and even now he does not like to discuss this topic with his comrades. He thinks that he is able to see every object again in its original form and color. But it takes him a certain while to develop it. After this development, however, it is definitely localized. It is possible to perceive it in peripheral vision. It *is* there even if he looks away. That does, however, not exclude the fact that he can cause movements of his AB. He is able to change the size of objects intentionally.

Wen. His grandmother hears voices and believes that spirits are speaking to her; she was "always spiritualistically inclined." He thinks that his mother also has optical and acoustic "illusions." His brother and sister have a strong phantasy. When he was a child he also noticed voices. He went then to his mother and asked her about the matter. Even now when he is very excited he thinks that he hears voices. One evening he was waiting for his mother who was attending a lecture. Suddenly he heard her mounting the staircase and unlocking the door. But he waited in vain; she did not come.

When he was a child he very often saw his mother lying on a couch in his room. Her appearance troubled him very much. Once he was hunting and shot an "animal" but discovered that it was the trunk of a tree. He thinks that he can draw very well and can go on drawing after the object is taken away. Then he sees there certain details he did not notice before.

Suh. He sees sometimes the faces of persons he knows very well. He reports about AB of flowers and of objects he uses in the chemical laboratory. In certain cases the AB appear without effort on his part, sometimes effort is required.

Ret. He sees especially objects with light colors; e. g.
flowers. They have the original color. Sometimes
the AB appear spontaneously. One day he was
thinking about the design of a toolcase. Suddenly
the AB of a tool-case which was different from
all cases he ever saw before appeared before him.
He placed the AB on the floor and was able to
make the design. This AB-case was gray, the case
he made was painted green. Since he often has to
do with furniture design his gift helps him a great
deal.

Dem. She often sees colors which do not belong to definite objects. These colors appear chiefly in peripheral vision. The objects she is looking at are
sometimes covered with different shades which
rapidly change. She sees a blue rim parallel to
the border on the wall. When she enters a room
the heads of the persons present are surrounded
by colors: red, green, yellow, but especially blue.
The same individual has, however, not always the
same color. The head of the E e. g. on some
occasions is surrounded by a white, on other days
by light yellow. The fingers and arms have also
this rim. In general, the whole world seems
"fluctuating and vibrating." She thinks that "a
state of not being concentrated, a relaxed mind"
considerably favors these phenomena. Before the
beginning of the experiments she consistently "sup-
pressed" these phenomena and succeeded. She men-
tions the power of "concentration" several times.
Now, however, she sometimes tries to get the colors
at will. One morning she sees green. After its disappearance she is successful in getting the color
again.—She sees a pencil surrounded with a blue
shade. E makes it disappear gradually behind a
ground. The moment the edge of the pencil is
entirely covered by the paper the blue flits to the
coat of the E.—She is not only able to cause the

disappearance of these subjective phenomena, but also to "blot out" objective colors. An intense blue square which is lying on a black ground is finally covered by the surrounding color; but the contour can be recognized. A long process of concentration, however, is necessary to make red colors disappear.

S also reports that she sees images in the hypnagogic state. Sometimes she hears voices and gets pleasant and unpleasant odors, but is unable to discover any definite causes for them. It is very surprising to her that she gets extremely pleasant odors she never perceived in reality. She does not suppress these phenomena but enjoys them.

The S is majoring in philosophy and has heard of Rudolph Steiner. Upon the question why some of her AB are more distinct than others she describes 3 different ways of getting very clear phenomena. 1. "I look at the object with a certain intensity. I notice every detail, every proportion. etc. And afterwards I have a clear image." 2. "I look at an object without any special attention. In spite of it I get a wonderfully distinct image." 3. "A peculiar act of concentration is necessary. I have then a feeling in my head as if I were studying hard. It is as if a light and diffused something gets centered and crystallized. It all comes together. Just as if it were swallowed up by the brain."

Rin.   She has seen different objects, especially faces of persons "who appeal to me." She reports about the appearance of a friend who went east. Sometimes she saw pictures again. "I was always a dreamer. That is the way I amuse myself." One day she remarks that she sees the dresses of women in the complementary color. "I never noticed that before. Your experiments made me conscious."

Seh.   In a very talkative way she reports about the vividness of her visual images in general. She thinks
herself to have a very good visual memory. She
recognized a man in Market Street, San Francisco,
who was working for her husband 12-14 years
ago. Her husband, who was with her, could not
even remember the fact that the man she was talk-
ing about had done work for him. Her AB arise
spontaneously or at will. Thus, e. g. she was
thinking about a problem in an examination. Certain questions were on the blackboard. Suddenly
she saw the answer written in an empty place on
the board. She is very musical; hearing a certain
melody she at once gets the "corresponding" visual
MI; e. g. if it is a gay melody she sees perhaps
a wonderful bright landscape. Then it is impossible to see anything sad. Once a foreign com-
poser whose work she was playing before him
was much surprised that she could express the
inner life of the melody so remarkably. She believes that is only due to the fact that she is always
forced to transform the acoustic material into optical MI. S has, however, no sound photisms. Seh
is her daughter, and she reports her 6 year old
child has the same gift.

Lin.   She thinks that her AB never arise spontaneously;
preliminary "hard thinking" is necessary. Once
in such a state of concentration she saw the answer
on the blackboard. (See Urbantschitsch's experiments.)

Jus.   He sometimes had seen beautiful flowers and
pictures. Once a cowboy riding horseback passed
him. After his disappearance he saw the whole
action again. The horse was quite distinct, the
rider "somewhat squashed in." (Compare Freiling 15, p. 124).

Low.   His remarks show that he sharply distinguishes
between MI and visualization. He has not made

many previous observations. Once he saw two birds sitting before the house.

Nit. Sometimes it happened that she saw the face of a friend in AB. When E asks her to visualize the ink bottle she has at home, she tries but remarks finally: "I can imagine that I can see it, but I cannot see it here."

Nak. She reports with great assurance that she once saw the face of her mother, once a dog and one day a horse. "This horse was smaller, but it was a real horse. It had the same color and form." After a drawing lesson she often sees the forms on the wall.

Maq. He thinks that "hard thinking" is necessary to get AB. He can place the object where he wants to and believes that he can see every object. He sees the face of his mother very plainly if he wants to.

Laj. She thinks that it is possible for her to see every object again. "But I have to think about it, then I get it."

Sel. She thinks "everybody can do that." In the grades it was sometimes very amusing to look at pictures, etc., in the AB. In the sixth or seventh grade she wrote a story where she personified inanimate objects.

Sut. She sometimes sees faces in her own room which were in most cases not known to her. Then she is very much surprised.

Gil. She sees different objects, faces, flowers, or perhaps a dress. Her mother reports that she herself when she was a ten year old child saw faces so plainly that she could draw them if she projected them on a background.

The S whose past extra-laboratory experiences have been reviewed cannot recall in most cases the exact form, color and duration of the phenomena observed. Moreover it is not possible for the E to check exactly the specific character of the phenomena in question. But even so these reports are quite valuable.

1. In general, the statements of the observers hardly differ in the majority of cases from those reported in the Marburg publications. (Compare also Fischer-Hirschberg (14) and Zeman (100). It seems natural that the reports of children are so much shorter than those of adults.

Aside from the youth of these observers it must be noted that the AB are probably more closely linked up with the whole mental life and therefore not considered to be "queer."

2. The reports illustrate quite well the different circumstances under which AB in everyday life may arise. Some light is thrown on the method of "getting" AB. (See especially Dem's three methods.)

3. "Manches der von uns im Vorhergehenden beschriebenen Bilder würde von psychiatrischer Seite aus unbedenklich als Halluzination, mindestens als Pseudohalluzination, angesprochen werden können. Wenn mit einer solchen Terminologie nicht der Vorwurf geistiger Erkrankung verbunden ist, so braucht man um den Namen nicht zu streiten." (Kroh 67, p. 161.)

The examinations of the statements of our observers will undoubtedly lead to the same conclusion which Kroh reached after his investigation of the material concerning certain German authors. In fact, if one keeps in mind the above stated qualification of Kroh an AB might properly be called pseudohallucination. (Fischer and Hirschberg also reach the conclusion that AB and pseudohallucinations have much in common.) An individual having AB is, of course, not necessarily pathological; but a pathological person might very well have AB. The psychologist who is going to investigate eidetic appearances *has to do with AB in either case.* He will possibly find that the AB differ phenomenologically. But if he does not stick to methodological presuppositions like those of Jaensch there is no reason to exclude a certain group of AB. Therefore in this study cases are included where the AB sometimes show a behavior which readily might be called apsychonomic. Succinctly stated: there are no normal and abnormal AB, but only normal and abnormal possessors of AB. Their AB, however, may present recognizable differences, and these differences may some day become, as Kroh has pointed out, indices for prepsychotic states.

The responses of Dem are sometimes characterized by a certain meaninglessness. Certain forms (especially with closed eyes) and colors which are not conditioned by outer stimuli and whose appearance seems quite unexpected to the S remind one of the appearances observed by Fritz B, one of Jaensch's subjects. (38, p. 174.) Jaensch thinks that we have here to do with the AB of a "schizoid type." (He found only one case in his whole material.) In the majority of her observations, however, Dem describes AB whose character does not differ very much from the AB in our material. In general it seems quite possible to learn something about the mental life of psychotic personalities by investigating their AB. (Schizophrenia.)

Even if one takes into account the character of the AB as "pseudohallucinations" there seem to be certain cases in our material where one gets the impression that the eidetic disposition is flourishing on pathological soil.

Hallucinations and illusions in different sense fields have occurred to these persons. Cases of this kind are seemingly Dem and Wen. In general on the basis of our observations we have no reason to doubt Jaensch's hypothesis that in all cases (or at least almost all cases) the eidetic gift of an adult represents "a youth endowment." At the same time in certain cases the presence of AB, even in children, may prove symptomatic of latent or overt mental disorders.

5. *THE EIDETIC DISPOSITION WITH REFERENCE TO CERTAIN SPECIAL PROBLEMS*

A. *Relation to intelligence.*

According to Jaensch the possession of AB is neither an advantage nor a disadvantage. The eidetic gift in *itself* has, so to speak, no positive or negative value. Thus he expects that the difference between two Eidetiker, say between Goethe and a man belonging to a primitive race is just the difference between—Goethe and a man belonging to such a race.

However, even if one takes it for granted that the eidetic disposition of adults is in *all* cases a heritage from the days of childhood nevertheless one might expect that the function which this disposition has within the whole mental life of an adult differs from the role it has with children. Our observations concerning the relationship between the eidetic disposition and the factor generally called intelligence seem to indicate that there really is a *difference* between these two groups in this respect. The children we used were according to the teachers' judgment average or good pupils. An examination of the school records seemed to show the same. Sel even belongs to Terman's group of "gifted children." Some of the children, however, were characterized as "dreamers"; they needed help at home to follow the lessons.

The *adults* from the State Teachers College, San Jose, —Rin, Leh, Kas, Lin and Ret—were designated as "queer and odd people" by one of the teachers, but so far as intelligence is concerned Rin and Ret seem to be at least average.

For most of the adults from Stanford University Thorndike Scores were available: Zeh 66.36; Wel 67.6; Mar 64.74; Wen 48.32; Suh 63.72; Ton 53.5; Bec 75.63. Dem, Lil and Ber—the first two very strong cases, the latter very weak—seem to be fairly good students; but no scores could be obtained for them.

In general, on the basis of our material one gets the impression that in the case of adult Eidetiker one is likely not to find a high IQ.

B. *Relation to somatic* basis.

Henning, as well as Koffka, decline to discuss the hypotheses of W. Jaensch concerning the B-, T- and BT-type since the value of this theory can be determined only on medical grounds. (Fischer and Hirschberg in the meantime tried to determine this value from medical standpoint. Their results do not confirm W. Jaensch's conclusions. See, however, 105)

If one should speak in terms of Jaensch's theory about our material one would expect the incidence of BT-types in this district. The amount of calcium in the different wells which furnish the drinking water for these localities differs considerably. According to information obtained from the chemical laboratory of Stanford University we have at least average values compared with other districts. (According to W. Jaensch the AB_T disappear due to the effect of high calcium content in drinking water.) The iodine content is comparatively high.

6. *SUMMARY*.

The conclusions based on the experiments are indicated on pp. 183-210. Some general remarks must be added.

An examination of the characteristics of the AB of our material as brought out in our experimental work seems to show that we had to do with Eidetiker who stand *between* the cases of Jaensch and Urbantschitsch. In the majority of cases the AB have neither the "regular" behavior of the Marburg AB nor the "irregular" behavior of the Vienna AB.[1] With such material it is hardly possible to *solve* the problems of perceptual psychology convincingly. It is possible, however, (1) to determine the characteristics of eidetic vision, and our work is a contribution toward the solution of this problem; (2) to determine the relation between eidetic disposition and Eidetiker, and our work has thrown light upon this relation too.

Many of the experimental results of the Marburg School have been confirmed. It is not possible for us, however, to accept the theory which is directing the experimental work of this school. In general, we think it wholly impossible to throw light upon matters of so general a nature as those dealt with by Jaensch. The results of investigations e. g. concerning the tendency of invariance in the perceptual world, however thorough they may be will never carry weight in the discussion

---

[1]So far as the frequency is concerned the district studied here seems to have at least the same percentage of Eidetiker as Marburg.

of invariance in a logical sense. We do not see how it is possible to establish a relation between Cassirer's[2] "Reihenbegriff" and certain processes in the eidetic field. Fortunately, the value of the Marburg studies does not depend upon considerations as to what constitutes logic, since these studies are "innerhalb der Kontinuität des streng systematischen Entwicklungszuges unseres Faches." And this continuity explains why the Marburg School speaks of the eidetic type chiefly in terms of spatial psychological investigations. (With regard to the problem of psychological types in general, see pp. 57-59).

Some problems for further research might be suggested:

1. A systematic study of the eidetic disposition at different age levels.

2. A study of the pre-school child with reference to Krellenberg's "unitary type."

3. A study of the eidetic disposition in different localities in America.

4. The influence of various methods of instruction upon the eidetic disposition.

5. The eidetic disposition in different racial groups.

6. The influence of different occupations upon the eidetic disposition.

7. The eidetic disposition with reference to questions of vocational guidance.

8. The eidetic disposition with reference to thinking, memory, emotional life, etc.

---

[2]Cassirer, E. Substanzbegriff und Funktionsbegriff. Untersuchungen über die Grundfragen der Erkenntniskritik. Berlin: Bruno Cassirer, 1910. Pp. 459.

9. The relation of the eidetic disposition to various levels of motor activity.

10. The eidetic disposition in various sense fields.

11. Eidetic disposition: its bearing on abnormal psychology and animal psychology.

It goes without saying that eidetic research bears upon most problems of perceptual psychology.

BIBLIOGRAPHY

1. Alexander, H. B.   Some observations on visual imagery. Psychol. Rev., 1904, *11*, 319.

2. Allport, G. W.   Eidetic imagery. Brit. J. Psychol., 1924, *15*, 99.

3. Blachowski, S.   Studien über den Binnenkontrast. Zsch. f. Sinnesphysiol., 1913, *47*, 291.

4. Bocci, B.   L'immagine visiva cerebrale. Contributo all' ottico fisiologica. Roma, 1897

5. Busse, P.   Über die Gedächtnisstufen und ihre Beziehung zum Aufbau der Wahrnehmungswelt. Zsch. f. Psychol., 1920. *84*, 1.

6. Cassirer, E.   Substanzbegriff und Funktionsbegriff. Untersuchungen über die Grundfragen der Erkenntniskritik. Berlin: Bruno Cassirer, 1910. Pp. 459.

7. Coover, J. E.   Experiments in psychical research, 1917. Leland Stanford Junior University Publications. Psychical Research Monograph No. 1, pp. 411-438.

8. Dimmick, C. C.   The auditory memory after-image. Amer. J. Psychol., 1923, *34*, 1.

9. Downey, J. E.   On the reading and writing of mirror-script. Psychol. Rev., 1914, *21*, 408.

10. Ellis, H.   Mescal, a study of a divine plant. Pop. Science Monthly, 1902, *61*, 52.

11. Exner, S.   Studien auf dem Grenzgebiete des lokalisierten Sehens. Arch. f. d. ges. Physiol., 1898, *73*, 117.

12. Fechner, Th.   Eelemente der Psychophysik. Leipzig, 1889.

13. Fernberger, S. W.   Observations on taking peyote. (Anhalonium Lewinii). Amer. J. Psychol, 1923, *34*, 267, 616.

14. Fischer, S. & Hirschberg, H. Die Verbreitung der eidetischen Anlage im Jugendalter und ihre Beziehungen zu körperlichen Merkmalen. Zsch. f. d. ges. Neurol. u. Psychiat., 1924, *88*, 241.

15. Freiling, H. Über die räumlichen Wahrnehmungen der Jugendlichen in der eidetischen Entwicklungsphase. Zsch. f. Sinnesphysiol., 1923, *55*, 69.

16. Freiling H., Jaensch, E. R., & Reich, F. Das Kovariantenphänomen, mit Bezug auf die allgemeinen Struktur und Entwicklungsfragen der räumlichen Wahrnehmungen. Zsch. f. Sinnesphysiol., 1923, *55*, 47.

17. Fuchs, W. Experimentelle Untersuchungen über die Aenderung von Farben unter dem Einfluss von Gestalten. ("Angleichungserscheinungen.") Zsch. f. Psychol., 1923, *92*, 249.

18. Galton, F. Inquiries into human faculty and its development. London: MacMillan & Co., 1883. Pp. XII + 380.

19. Goldschmidt, R. H. Grössenschwankungen gestaltfester, urbildverwandter Nachbilder und der Emmertsche Satz. Arch. f. d. ges. Psychol., 1923, *44*, 51.

20. Gösser, A. Über die Gründe des verschiedenen Verhaltens der einzelnen Gedächtnisstufen. Zsch. f. Psychol., 1921, *87*, 97.

21. Gottheil, E. Über das latente Sinnengedächtnis der Jugendlichen und seine Aufdeckung. Zsch. f. Psychol., 1921, *87*, 73.

22. Guttmann, A. Experimentelle Halluzinationen durch Anhalonium Lewini. Schumann: Bericht über den VI. Kongress für exp. Psych. 1914.

23. Helmholtz, H. Handbuch der physiologischen Optik. 1909. Hamburg und Leipzig: L. Voss.

24. Henning, H. Starre eidetische Klang-und Schmerzbilder und die eidetische Konstellation. Zsch. f. Psychol., 1923, *92*, 137.

25. Henning, H. Neue Typen der Vorstellungsbilder und die Entwicklung des Vorstellens. Zsch. f. angew. Psychol., 1923, *22*, 387.

26. Hering, E. Über das Gedächtnis als eine allgemeine Funktion der organischen Materie. Ostwald's "Klassiker der exakten Naturwissenschaften." 148.

27. Herwig, B.   Über den inneren Farbensinn der Ju-
                          gendlichen und seine Beziehung zu
                          den allgemeinen Fragen des Lichtsinns.
                          Zsch. f. Psychol., 1921, 87, 129.
28. Herwig, B. &   Über Mischung von objektiv darge-
    Jaensch, E. R.   botenen Farben mit Farben des An-
                          schauungsbildes. Zsch. f. Psychol.,
                          1921, 87, 217.
29. Hibbert-Ware, S.   Sketches of the philosophy of appari-
                          tions. Edinburgh: Oliver & Boyd,
                          1825. Pp. 475.
30. Jaensch, E. R.   Zur Analyse der Gesichtswahrnehmun-
                          gen. Experimentell-psychologische Un-
                          tersuchungen nebst Anwendung auf
                          die Pathologie des Sehens. Zsch. f.
                          Psychol., 1909, Ergänzungsband 4.
31. Jaensch. E. R.   Über die Wahrnehmung des Raumes.
                          Eine experimentell-psychologische Un-
                          tersuchung nebst Anwendung auf
                          Asthetik und Erkenntnislehre. Zsch. f.
                          Psychol., 1911, Ergänzungsband 6.
32. Jaensch, E. R.   Die experimentelle Analyse der An-
                          schauungsbilder als Hilfsmittel zur Un-
                          tersuchung der Wahrnehmungs-und
                          Denkvorgänge. Sitzungsbericht d. Ges.
                          zur Beförderung d. ges. Naturwiss. z.
                          Marburg, 1917.
33. Jaensch, E. R.   Zur Methodik experimenteller Unter-
                          suchungen an optischen Anschauungs-
                          bildern. Zsch. f. Psychol., 1920, 85, 37.
34. Jaensch, E. R.   Über Kontrast im optischen Anschau-
                          ungsbild. Zsch. f. Psychol., 1921, 87, 211.
35. Jaensch, E. R.   Über den Nativismus in der Lehre von
                          der Raumwahrnehmung. Zsch. f. Sin-
                          nesphysiol., 1921, 52, 229.
36. Jaensch, E. R.   Über die subjektiven Anschauungs-
                          bilder. Bericht über den VII. Kon-
                          gress für exp. Psych. in Marburg, 1922.
37. Jaensch, E. R.   Zur Richtigstellung und Ergänzung.
                          Zsch. f. Psychol., 1922, 88, 317.
38. Jaensch, E. R.   Uber Raumverlagerung und die Bezïe-
                          hung von Raumwahrnehmung und
                          Handeln. Zsch. f. Psychol., 1922, 89,
                          116.
39. Jaensch, E. R.   Die Völkerkunde und der eidetische
                          Tatsachenkreis. Zsch. f. Psychol.,
                          1922, 91, 88.
40. Jaensch, E. R.   Übergang zu einer Schichtenanalyse
                          des Bewusstseins und einiger seiner
                          Substrate, gegründet auf die Struk-

turanalyse der eidetischen Entwicklungsschicht. Zsch. f. Psychol., 1922, *91*, 83.

41. Jaensch, E. R.   Beziehungen von Erlebnisanalyse und Sprachwissenschaft, erläutert an den Verben der sinnlichen Wahrnehmung. Zsch. f. Psychol., 1923, *91*, 343.

42. Jaensch, E. R.   Der Umbau der Wahrnehmungslehre und die Kantischen Weltanschauungen. Zsch. f. Psychol., 1923, *92*, 1.

43. Jaensch, E. R.   Wahrnehmungslehre und Biologie. Zsch. f. Psychol., 1923, *93*, 129.

44. Jaensch, E. R.   Über den Aufbau der Wahrnehmungswelt und ihre Struktur im Jugendalter. Leipzig: Barth. 1923. Pp. XXIV + 567.

45. Jaensch, E. R.   Über Gegenwartsaufgaben der Jugendpsychologie. Zsch. f. Psychol., 1924, *94*, 38.

46. Jaensch, E. R.   Die Eidetik und die typologische Forschungsmethode in ihrer Bedeutung für die Jugendkunde und Pädagogik, für die allgemeine Psychologie und die Psychophysiologie der menschlichen Persönlichkeit Zsch. f. päd. Psych., 1924, *26*, 37, 202, 236.

47. Jaensch, E. R.   Alois Riehl, der Mann und das Werk. Kantstudien 1925, *30*, V.

48. Jaensch, E. R. & W.   Über die Verbreitung der eidetischen Anlage im Jugendalter. Zsch. f. Psychol., 1921, *87*, 91.

49. Jaensch, E. R. & Reich, F.   Über die Lokalisation im Sehraum. Zsch. f. Psychol., 1921, *86*, 278.

50. Jaensch, W.   Über psychophysische Konstitutionstypen. Monatssch. f. Kinderheilkunde, 1921, *22*, Heft 2.

51. Jaensch, W.   Über psychophysische Konstitutionstpyen. Münch. med. Woch., 1921, 68.

52. Jaensch, W.   Über psychophysische Konstitutionstypen. Münch. med. Woch., 1922, 69.

53. James, W.   The principles of psychology. New York: Holt & Co., Vol. I & II, 1890.

54. Kandinsky.   Kritische und klinische Betrachtungen im Gebiete der Sinnestäuschungen. 1885.

55. Katz, D   Die Erscheinungsweisen der Farben. Zsch. f. Psychol. 1911. Ergänzungsband VII.

56. Kerschensteiner, G. M. A. Die Entwicklung der zeichnerischen Begabung. München, C. Gerber, 1905. Pp. 508.

57. Klüver, H. Psychological and sociological types. Psychol. Rev., 1924, *31*, 456.

58. Klüver, H. The problem of type in "cultural science psychology." J. of Philos., 1925, *22*, 225.

59. Klüver, H. An analysis of recent work on the problem of psychological types. J. of Nerv. & Ment. Dis. 1925, *62*, 561.

60. Koffka, K. Zur Analyse der Vorstellungen und ihrer Gesetze. Leipzig: Quelle & Meyer 1912. Pp. VI + 392.

61. Koffka, K. Über die Untersuchungen an den sogenannten optischen Anschauungsbildern. Psychol. Forschung. 1923, *3*, 124.

62. Koffka, K. Über die Messung der Grösse von Nachbildern. Psychol. Forschung., 1923, 3, 219.

63. Koffka, K. The growth of the mind. 1924. Pp. XVI + 383.

64. Köhler, W. Intelligenzprüfungen an Anthropoiden. I. Abh. d. Preuss. Ak. d. Wiss., 1917. Physikalisch-math. Klasse.

65. Köhler, W. Die physischen Gestalten in Ruhe und im stationären Zustand. Braunschweig: Vieweg & Sohn, 1920. Pp. XX + 263.

66. Krellenberg, P. Über die Herausdifferenzierung der Wahrnehmungs-und Vorstellungswelt aus der originären eidetischen Einheit. Zsch. f. Psychol., 1922, *88*, 56.

67. Kroh, O. Eidetiker unter deutschen Dichtern. Zsch. f. Psychol., 1920, *85*, 118.

68. Kroh, O. Subjektive Anschauungsbilder bei Jugendlichen. Eine psychologisch-pädagogische Untersuchung. Göttingen: Vandenhoeck & Ruprecht, 1922. Pp. VIII + 195.

69. Kroh, O. Subjektive optische Anschauungsbilder bei Jugendlichen. Zsch. f. päd. Psychol., 1922, *23*, 40.

70. Kroh, O. Die eidetische Anlage bei Jugendlichen. Zsch. f. Kinderforschung 1924, *29*, 63.

71 Kröncke, K. Zur Phänomenologie der Kernfläche des Sehraums. Zsch. f. Sinnesphysiol., 1921, *52*, 217.

72. Külpe, O.   Über die Objektiverung und Subjektivierung von Sinneseindrücken. Phil. Studien, 1902, *18*, 508.

73. Martin, L. J.   Die Projektionsmethode und die Lokalisation visueller und anderer Vorstellungsbilder. Zsch. f. Psychol., 1912, *61*, 321.

74. Martin, L. J.   Quantitative Untersuchungen über das Verhältnis unanschaulicher Bewusstseinsinhalte. Zsch. f. Psychol., 1913, *65*, 417.

75. Martin, L. J.   Über die Abhängigkeit visueller Vorstellungsbilder vom Denken. Zsch. f. Psychol., 1914-15, *70*, 212.

76. Mayerhausen, G. Noch einmal der gefässlose Bezirk der menschlichen Retina. Arch. f. Ophth., 1883, *29*, 150.

77. Meyer, G. H.   Physiologie der Nervenfaser. 1843.

78. Mochi, A.   Neueste Untersuchungen über die Projektion monokularer Nachbilder durch das nichtbelichtete Auge. Zsch. f. Sinnesphysiol., 1910, *44*, 81.

79. Müller, G. E.   Zur Analyse der Gedächtnistätigkeit und des Vorstellungsverlaufs. Zsch. f. Psychol., 1911, Ergänzungsband V; 1913, Ergänzungsband VIII; 1917, Ergänzungsband IX.

80. Müller, J.   Über die phantastischen Gesichtserscheinungen. 1826.

81. Newberne, R. E. Peyote. Chilocco, Oklahoma, 1923.
    L. & Burke, C. H.

82. Parish, E.   Hallucinations and illusions, a study of the fallacies of perception. 1877. Pp. 390.

83. Perky, C. W.   An experimental study of imagination. Am. J. Psychol., 1910, *21*, 422.

84. Rieffert, J.   Über die Objektivierung und Subjektivierung von Sinneseindrücken. Schumann: Bericht über den V. Kongress f. exp. Psych. 1912.

85. Scharwin, W. &   Über den scheinbaren Grössenwechsel
    Novizki, A.   der Nachbilder im Auge. Zsch. f. Psychol., 1896, *11*, 408.

86. Schrenk, J.   Über das Verständnis für bildliche Darstellung bei Schulkindern. Leipzig, 1914.

87. Schwab, G.   Vorläufige Mitteilung über die Untersuchungen zum Wesen der subjektiven

		Anschauungsbilder. Psych. Forsch. 1924, *5*, 321.
88.	Seashore, C. E.	Measurements of illusions and hallucinations in normal life. Studies fr. the Yale Psychol. Lab., New Haven, 1895, III.
89.	Staudenmaier, L.	Die Magie als experimentelle Naturwissenschaft. 1916.
90.	Stern, W.	Die Aussage als geistige Leistung und Verhörsprodukt. Beiträge zur Psychologie der Aussage I. Leipzig: Barth, 1903-04. Pp. 541.
91.	Stern, W.	Über verlagerte Raumformen. Zsch. f. angew. Psychol. 1909, *2*.
92.	Stern, W.	Psychology of early childhood, New York: H. Holt, 1924.
93.	Stratton, G. M.	The mnemonic feat of the "Shass Pollak." Psychol. Rev., 1917, *24*, 244.
94.	Stumpf, C.	Empfindung und Vorstellung. Abh. d. Preuss. Adad. d. Wiss. 1918. Philos.-Historische Klasse.
95.	Urbantschitsch, V.	Über die Beeinflussung subjektiver Gesichtsempfindungen. Arch. f. d. ges. Physiol., 1903, *94*, 347.
96.	Urbantschitsch, V.	Über Sinnesempfindungen und Gedächtnisbilder. Arch. f. d. ges. Physiol., 1905, *110*, 437.
97.	Urbantschitsch, V.	Über subjektive optische Anschauungsbilder. Leipzig und Wien: F. Deuticke, 1907. Pp. VI + 211.
98.	Urbantschitsch, V.	Über subjektive Hörerscheinungen und subjektive optische Anschauungsbilder. 1908.
99.	Warren, H. C.	Some unusual visual after-effects. Psychol. Rev., 1921, *28*, 453.
100.	Zeman, H.	Verbreitung und Grad der eidetischen Anlage. Zsch. f. Psychol., 1924, *96*, 209.
101.	Zillig, M.	Über eidetische Anlage und Intelligenz. Fortschr. d. Psychol., 1922, *5*, 293.
Compare also:		
102.	Feyerabend, O.	Der innere Farbensinn der jugendlichen in seiner Beziehung zu der angenäherten Farbenkonstanz der Sehdinge. Zsch. f. Psychol. 1924, *94*, 209 and 1924, *95*, 85.
103.	Henning, H.	Das Urbild. Zsch. f. Psychol., 1924, *94*, 273.
104.	Henning, H.	Ausgeprägte Anschauungsbilder der

beiden Arten von Geschmackssinn. Zsch. f. Psychol., 1924, *95*, 137.

105. Jaensch, W.   Über psychophysische Konstitutionstypen. Zsch. f. d. ges. Neurol. & Psych., 1925, *97*, 374.

106. Scola, F.   Über das Verhältnis von Vorstellungsbild, Anschauungsbild und Nachbild. Arch. f. d. ges. Psychol., 1925, *52*, 297.

Classics In
Child Development

An Arno Press Collection

Baldwin, James Mark. **Thought and Things.** Four vols. in two.
1906-1915

Blatz, W[illiam] E[met], et al. **Collected Studies on the Dionne
Quintuplets.** 1937

Bühler, Charlotte. **The First Year of Life.** 1930

Bühler, Karl. **The Mental Development of the Child.** 1930

Claparède, Ed[ouard]. **Experimental Pedagogy and the
Psychology of the Child.** 1911

Factors Determining Intellectual Attainment. 1975

First Notes by Observant Parents. 1975

Freud, Anna. **Introduction to the Technic of Child Analysis.**
1928

Gesell, Arnold, et al. **Biographies of Child Development.** 1939

Goodenough, Florence L. **Measurement of Intelligence By
Drawings.** 1926

Griffiths, Ruth. **A Study of Imagination in Early Childhood
and Its Function in Mental Development.** 1918

Hall, G. Stanley and Some of His Pupils. **Aspects of Child Life
and Education.** 1907

Hartshorne, Hugh and Mark May. **Studies in the Nature of
Character. Vol. I: Studies in Deceit; Book One, General
Methods and Results.** 1928

Hogan, Louise E. **A Study of a Child.** 1898

Hollingworth, Leta S. **Children Above 180 IQ, Stanford Binet:** Origins and Development. 1942

Kluver, Heinrich. **An Experimental Study of the Eidetic Type.** 1926

Lamson, Mary Swift. **Life and Education of Laura Dewey Bridgman, the Deaf, Dumb and Blind Girl.** 1881

Lewis, M[orris] M[ichael]. **Infant Speech:** A Study of the Beginnings of Language. 1936

McGraw, Myrtle B. **Growth: A Study of Johnny and Jimmy.** 1935

Monographs on Infancy. 1975

O'Shea, M. V., editor. **The Child: His Nature and His Needs.** 1925

Perez, Bernard. **The First Three Years of Childhood.** 1888

Romanes, George John. **Mental Evolution in Man:** Origin of Human Faculty. 1889

Shinn, Milicent Washburn. **The Biography of a Baby.** 1900

Stern, William. **Psychology of Early Childhood Up to the Sixth Year of Age.** 1924

Studies of Play. 1975

Terman, Lewis M. **Genius and Stupidity:** A Study of Some of the Intellectual Processes of Seven "Bright" and Seven "Stupid" Boys. 1906

Terman, Lewis M. **The Measurement of Intelligence.** 1916

Thorndike, Edward Lee. **Notes on Child Study.** 1901

Wilson, Louis N., compiler. **Bibliography of Child Study.** 1898-1912

[Witte, Karl Heinrich Gottfried]. **The Education of Karl Witte,** Or the Training of the Child. 1914